The \

NOF

SN(

The Snowdon range from Cnicht ⌖

THE
VISITOR'S GUIDE TO
NORTH WALES
and SNOWDONIA

MPC

HUNTER
PUBLISHING INC

British Library Cataloguing in
Publication Data:
Macdonald, Colin
   The visitor's guide to North
   Wales. - 2nd ed.
   1. North Wales - Visitor's guides
   I. Title
   914.29'104858

Cover photograph: *Conwy Castle and
Telford's suspension Bridge* (International Photobank, Peter Baker)

Illustrations have been supplied by:
C. Barnes: p 136; J. P. Walker: p 159.
All other photographs are by the author
and from the MPC Picture Collection.

1st Edition   1982
2nd Edition (fully revised and
redesigned)   1989

Published by:
Moorland Publishing Co Ltd,
Moor Farm Road,
Airfield Estate,
Ashbourne,
Derbyshire DE6 1HD
England

ISBN 0 86190 293 9 (paperback)
ISBN 0 86190 292 0 (hardback)

Published in the USA by:
Hunter Publishing Inc,
300 Raritan Centre Parkway,
CN 94, Edison, NJ 08818

ISBN 1 55650 118 8 (USA)

Colour and black & white
origination by:
Scantrans, Singapore
Printed in the UK by:
Richard Clay Ltd, Bungay, Suffolk

CONTENTS

Key to Symbols Used on Maps and in Text Margin

 Recommended walk

 Parkland

 Archaeological site

 Nature reserve/Animal interest

 Birdlife

 Garden

 Watersports

 Steam railway

 Church/ecclesiastical site

 Building of interest

 Castle/Fortification

 Museum/Art gallery

 Beautiful view/Scenery, Natural phenomenon

 Other place of interest

 Industrial Archaeology

Note on the maps

The maps drawn for each chapter, while comprehensive, are not designed to be used as route maps, but rather to locate the main towns, villages and places of interest. For exploration, visitors are recommended to use the 1:50,000 (approximately $1\frac{1}{4}$ in to the mile) Ordnance Survey 'Landranger' maps. The sheets covering the areas included in this book are shown on page 7. For greater detail the Ordnance Survey 'Outdoor Leisure' maps, which cover the area in four sheets at 1:25,000 ($2\frac{1}{2}$ in to one mile) are recommended. The area is also covered by the OS Tourist Map T10 *Snowdonia and Anglesey* at 1 in to 1 mile.

INDEX TO 1:50 000 MAPS OF GREAT BRITAIN

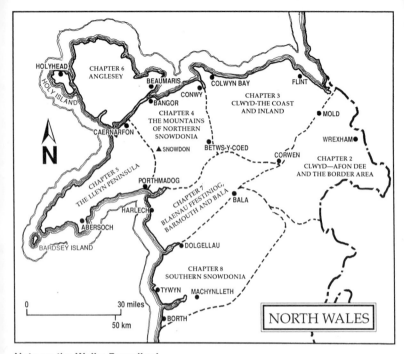

Note on the Walks Described

The walks in this book are not intended to be a field-by-field guide, but recommendations for the best routes. Many have been chosen so that they avoid the popular and crowded areas, while many are more interesting or give better views than the better-known routes. Walkers must be equipped according the the severity of the terrain: a lakeside stroll or woodland walk requires only stout shoes and weather protection. High level mountain walks need proper boots and clothing, map and compass and the ability to use them correctly

Mountain Recue

Telepone 999 and ask for Mountain Resue

For the walks in the text the distance and estimated time is given, together with the information below:

H	High level route for fine weather
M	Medium level route
L	Low level route, often recommended when the weather is poor
*	Well signposted and easily followed
**	Easy to follow with the aid of a map
***	Requires careful map reading
****	Recommended for experienced hill walkers only
†	Of least interest
††	
†††	
††††	Of most interest

INTRODUCTION

Arriving in North Wales for the first time most visitors will be agreeably surprised by the change of scenery. From the border counties of England the hills rise gradually from the plains, getting more rugged and grander the further one journeys west. The border counties are green and luxuriant, the western counties craggy and steep and although the mountains are not as high as their counterparts in other countries they are nevertheless quite impressive.

Many visitors will come solely to walk and climb in these hills, while many more will come for the glorious beaches that almost surround the region. Few parts of Great Britain are so accessible and can offer so much variety to the visitor; the combination of sea and mountains make it irresistable for many. One can be bathing on one of the many fine beaches and within the hour be heading for the summit of a mountain, though a change of dress would be recommended.

The larger coastal resorts offer excellent facilities for the tourist, good hotels, camping and caravan sites plus a range of activities for all ages. There has in recent years been an increase in visitor facilities besides the more traditional entertainments. You can go down a slate mine, make your own pottery, travel on a miniature railway, visit any number of museums, enjoy indoor watersports or go round a gaol. There is something for everyone. There is no need to be bored in North Wales.

Many first time visitors to the region will naturally head for the better known areas. However, a little in depth investigation will uncover a vast amount of history, places and detail that can only enhance your visit. The Welsh are naturally warm hearted and honest but they do expect these feelings to be reciprocated. The Welsh language should cause the visitor no problems as all who do speak Welsh also speak English. Road signs are now mainly in the Welsh form which in most cases is very similar to the earlier anglicised spelling. Welsh names are used where possible throughout this book, while the Ordnance Survey has been used as the mediator if any doubt has arisen.

For the purposes of this book North Wales is taken to be the northern counties of Clwyd and Gwynedd. Clwyd is that part of the north-east along the estuary of the Dee and adjoining the English counties of Cheshire and Shropshire; to the west it has the Afon Conwy as its boundary. It has more than 50 per cent of the population of the whole of the area and certainly most of the industry around Wrexham and along Deeside. It also contains the larger coastal resorts of Rhyl, Colwyn Bay and Llandudno. It too has its fair share of hills, castles and beauty spots. Close to the major cities of Liverpool and Manchester it is popular with day trippers.

To the west and bordering the Irish Sea is the county of Gwynedd, with its beautiful coastline, its rugged mountains and quieter resorts. The two counties are as different as chalk and cheese. The shared county boundary is almost like crossing another border, for Gwynedd has a far greater proportion of Welsh speakers and one always feels closer to Wales in Gwynedd. Gwynedd also has the Snowdonia National Park as its heartland, with much of the finest scenery and the highest mountains in Wales.

The island of Anglesey, or Ynys Mon, separated by the narrow straits from the north-west coast, gives this varied county a further dimension. Gwynedd is considered by many to be the heart of Wales, epitomising every aspect of the country and its culture.

Snowdonia is the name that for centuries has been given by travellers to the mountains in the old county of Caernarfonshire. In 1951 these, along with the ranges of mountains to the south and the

Sunset over Llynau Mymbyr and the Snowdon range

east were designated a National Park and the name Snowdonia was adopted as the official title of the park. As a park it extends from Conwy in the north to Aberdyfi in the south and from Bala in the east to Tremadog in the west, roughly 50 miles long and 35 miles wide though this does vary. Besides the mountains there are a multitude of lakes and 22 miles of coast are included with some of the finest beaches in Wales.

The National Park has fourteen peaks over 3,000ft with many more falling only a few feet short. The area is scantily populated by comparison with the adjacent counties and is almost purely Welsh speaking, it could be said that the sheep outnumber the people and even the sheepdogs only respond to commands given in Welsh.

Unlike National Parks in other parts of the world, Snowdonia and the other parks in Great Britain are all working areas. The people own the land, they work it and in most cases live on it. The balance between access for the visitor to any area within the park is generally with the goodwill of the landlord and care must always be taken to leave the area as you found it, so take nothing but memories and photographs.

You will find many beautiful areas in North Wales. If you enjoy peace and tranquility you can easily escape from the hustle and bustle of modern life. There are quiet little valleys, beaches and villages. The area is so compact it is not difficult to enjoy a varied holiday without travelling too far.

The area considered in this book has been divided into sub areas and each has a separate chapter. There are suggestions for places to visit, things to do and walks to enjoy. These are unlikely to be the only attractions available and a little individual exploration will uncover a wealth of hidden pleasures.

There are few, if any, properties (either National Trust or privately owned) that are open all year round. As many are open only on summer weekdays, it is always sensible to check visiting hours beforehand with the local Tourist Information Centres.

Some walks are suggested, and while most are fairly easy and can be tackled by the average person, many — particularly within Snowdonia — are more arduous and should not be attempted without due preparation. As the weather can change quickly, extra clothing and waterproofs should always be taken on a long walk. A map, too, adds so much to the enjoyment. A 1:50,000 Ordnance Survey map of the area will be invaluable. Many small areas and forests have their own nature trails or forest trails; individual leaflets are generally available at nearby information offices or shops.

Throughout this guide are suggestions for visits and walks, and at the end of the book is useful information for visitors. Every effort has been made to ensure the accuracy of the information and, though lack of space precludes much that may be of interest, it is hoped that visitors will use it as a basis for an enjoyable holiday.

1
NORTH WALES: A BACKGROUND

Wales is made up geologically of ancient hard rocks 200 million or more years old. Parts of Snowdonia and Anglesey consist, however, of much that is 650 million years old, some of the oldest rocks to be found anywhere in the world. The names of these extremely early geological epochs, such as the Cambrian, Ordovician and Silurian periods, as used by earth scientists throughout the world, are taken from the names of the early tribes that lived in Wales.

These rocks are hardwearing and resistant to erosion, and where they have been upthrust have resisted wear to leave us the mountains that are such a feature of the landscapes, though these are mere stumps of their predecessors. These hard volcanic rocks form the bulk of the western areas, while Clwyd and the lower hills in eastern areas are made up of softer sedimentary rocks, limestones and sandstones which stretch out towards England. These hills are more rounded, less craggy and gentler on the eye.

Formed by huge upthrusts that wrinkled the earth's surface many millions of years ago and worn low by huge sheets of ice that covered the area in subsequent years the hard igneous rocks of Snowdonia have survived to form the mountains we enjoy today. The evidence of this wearing is everywhere: the moraines high up in the cwms, the drumlins which the glaciers deposited and on the

Rhinogs the huge glacial erratics — the rocks left high and dry when the ice receded. It was this wearing by ice and by water that cut the deep valleys throughout the area.

Minerals were formed in pockets in the rock: coal, iron ore and lead in the east and copper in the mountains of Snowdonia and all were exploited by man. Layers of mud became compacted and hardened by intense pressure and heat to form slate in bands up to 40ft thick, which was later to be mined and quarried throughout the area. It is probable that when man first came to the area he knew little of this wealth below the surface, but later he left hardly a hill untouched by his scratchings in search of something to sell or exchange or make into something useful.

Man's first forays were probably to the coastlands where he could survive on a diet of fish supplemented by the occasional wild ox or reindeer he could catch. His camps were temporary and we know little of his lifestyle; some caves he occupied close to Prestatyn which have been excavated, suggest that he was itinerant and show evidence that he may have been around just after the last Ice Age, approximately 18,000 years ago.

The first real evidence of man's industry in North Wales are the stone axe 'factories' as at Craig Llywd above Penmaenmawr and Mynydd Rhiw on the Lleyn Peninsula. Examples of stone axes from here have been found throughout Great Britain, but whether they were traded, exchanged or bartered we will never know. They were certainly valued, perhaps they were the first souvenirs taken home by palaeolithic visitors to the country.

The land was mainly forests of pine and birch and what scant evidence is available from the stone age periods shows that early man favoured coastal sites, river banks or lakeside locations. Stone tools are occasionally found on these low lying areas.

Later visitors brought more advanced tools and domestic farm animals but it was not until the Bronze Age that any great impact was felt in the area. It was during this period that many of the surviving standing stones, hut circles and burial chambers were erected.

From around 1800BC to 500BC the Bronze Age people worked and traded in the area. However, they were gradually overrun by, or became intermingled with, a group of settlers from Europe bringing with them the techniques of iron working. These immi-grants were followed, in about 300BC, by the first Celts who arrived from Gaul and settled mainly in the western areas of the country. Besides bringing agricultural skills they are noteworthy for the many hillforts they built in Wales, Tre'r Ceiri on Yr Eifl being a fine example.

It is likely that the roots of Welsh culture and probably the language lay with this pre-Roman group of settlers, though it is difficult to pin down with complete certainty. Celtic undoubtedly formed the basis of the language used in many western areas of Britain and France around that time. There is a similarity with Gaelic in Scotland and Ireland and the Breton language in France.

The coming of the Romans in AD43 further pushed the Celts to the peninsulas and western areas of Britain, cutting them off even further from mainland influences. By AD78 the Romans had con-quered North Wales, though whether they ever subjugated the natives is doubtful. They built several forts as at *Deva* (Chester), used as the base for sorties into the hostile country. *Segontium* (Caernarfon) was the major base within Gwynedd with many smaller camps throughout the county. Many of the present roads follow the lines of early Roman roads. It is likely that the Roman influence was small and much of the activity was to maintain a presence and trade with the natives. There is evidence that during their occupation the Romans mined gold and copper and other minerals, particularly lead, in the eastern areas of Wales.

In the fourth century AD the Romans returned home to save their falling Empire and left the Celts to return to their former primitive life. They have, however, left some signs of their presence and though their forts were small they are fairly plentiful.

The next major influence came in the fifth and sixth centuries with the arrival of the first Christians from the Continent and Ireland. These priests and monks came to form the backbone of the Celtic Church and established many of the early churches, such as at St Asaph and Bangor. There was a post-Roman Christian movement and by the sixth century AD Celts had been converted from paganism to this new religion. The word was spread by itinerant saints who travelled the country creating religious settlements and building churches. The inclusion of 'Llan' coupled with the saint's name usually indicates such a place, such as Llanbadrig, The Church of Patrick, or Llandudno, The Church of St Tudno. Wales by the seventh century was fully converted and a major religious influence on the rest of the British Isles. There are many sites associated with those early wandering saints as at St Seriols Well close to Penmon Priory on Anglesey and St Beuno's Well (Ffynnon Beuno) at Clynnog on the Lleyn Peninsula.

The Norman invasion of England in 1066 was followed by the gradual conquest of Wales, though the principality of Gwynedd in the north formed an almost impregnable bastion of high hills and mountains. It was Edward I in the thirteenth century who systematically built a ring of steel in the form of castles at Flint, Rhuddan, Conwy, Beaumaris, Caernarfon and Harlech, all of which could be supplied by sea and all were virtually impregnable on the landward side. Edward strengthened some of the Welsh princes' castles at Criccieth and Dolwyddelan and was not only able to control the coastlands but also the very heartland of the country. It was Edward who anglicised the organisation of the country and named his eldest son the first Prince of Wales.

The native Welsh princes from then on fought a spasmodic rearguard action culminating with the abortive Owain Glyndwr revolt in the fifteenth century. There is a cave above Beddgelert on the slopes of Moel Hebog romantically associated with Glyndwr, which is said to be his hideaway during his escape. This was the last serious attempt to overthrow the English crown and subsequent to this the Welsh influence was purely cultural, with the language playing a major unifying role throughout the country.

The seventeenth century saw the industrial revolution arrive in North Wales with the mining of coal and iron around Wrexham, the mining of lead ore in the limestone hills in the north-east and copper in the mountains of Snowdonia. As you travel around you will see the great heaps of waste from some long dead mining operation, and there are few hillsides untouched by man's eager searches for profit.

Gwynedd is particularly rich in industrial archaeology, everywhere are the massive tips of the slate quarries and mines. North Wales is said to have roofed the world, providing much of the slate for the tremendous building projects during the industrial revolution.

The Eagle Tower, Caernarfon Castle, one of the castles built by Edward I to subdue the Welsh

The quarries are everywhere in the mountains, often on a huge scale, the mines have vast inner chambers where men worked in treacherous conditions for a pittance. The scale of these burrowings are often difficult to believe, particularly now all is quiet and little evidence remains of those who worked them.

Wild goats, although rare, may still be seen in Snowdonia

Ports developed around the coast specifically to handle the products from these enterprises, and were served by tramways and railways direct from mine to quay. For instance on the Ffestiniog-Porthmadog route, populations grew around both ends of the line and gradually the communities took shape. They are the villages and townships which exist today, but though the streets and houses are the same, economic conditions have changed. The mines and ports are closed, alternative work has had to be found or created, and while in most cases this has been successful, conditions can still be hard in the hills. The communities are still there, though depleted, vacant houses have been sold as weekend cottages as tourism has become a major industry. The old railways have been revived to carry tourists, the old mines are now museums, the ports

One of the many elegant stone bridges found in North Wales, this one over the Afon Croesor, with Cnicht — 'the Welsh Matterhorn' — in the background

cater for yachtsmen and fishermen, old crafts have been re-discovered and marketed, the hills are now being walked for leisure instead of necessity. The whole country has seen greater changes during the last 100 years than at any time during its previous history.

Today's visitor should take plenty of time to explore, and those who look deeper than the surface will find a wealth of interesting places to be discovered and so will enjoy their visit even more.

The Language

It is known with some certainty that the Celts who populated Britain from Europe in the fourth century BC brought not only their iron working skills but also their language. Those who arrived in Wales spoke Brythonic or a British language similar to that spoken in Brittany and Cornwall.

Pressures of the Roman invasion forced the Celtic people into the western areas of Britain where they became further isolated and the language began to develop on its own. In later centuries the subsequent invasion of the island by the Anglo-Saxons from Europe pushed the Celts into the extremes of the country, into Wales, Scotland and Cornwall.

During each occupation the developing language borrowed words freely from the invasion force and for much of the time they lived in peace. The language continued to adopt words from other invaders, Norman French through medieval English and right up to modern English. Other languages developed in a similar fashion.

Welsh was the main spoken language in the principality until the seventeenth century. The English influence, however, was spreading, as wealthy traders found it more convenient to be bilingual. English was also becoming used more widely for state purposes and as a public medium.

The church continued to use Welsh and through recent centuries has been the saviour of the language. Bishop Morgan had translated the Bible into Welsh in 1588 and this alone had ensured the survival of the language more than any other single act.

Nowadays many Welsh people are bilingual, particularly in western areas of the country like Gwynedd, less so in the border counties and on the northern coastlands where English is their first language. The Welsh language is taught to all pupils in school and

Most signposts are now both in Welsh and English

thankfully recent years have seen a swing to using the Welsh form on road signs and maps. There is now a widespread interest in the language and culture and though only a small proportion of the whole country is Welsh speaking, there is a revival in the customs and traditions of the country and much is being done to ensure the survival of the language.

The visitor to Wales will see place names that are different and will hear people speak in a very different language. This can be baffling to the non-Welsh speaker, while finding your way around can be a daunting task particularly if you have to ask your way.

Many place names are descriptive of the physical feature of the area, eg Moelwyn Mawr means the big bare hill. Others are named after the local church; hence the predominance of the names preceded by *Llan*, church of, as in Llanbadrig which means the church of Patrick. It can add interest and enjoyment to any holiday to try to solve the mystery of the language and find out where you are. A few words that may be useful are given overleaf; most are found in place names.

Aber — river mouth
Adwy — gap, pass
Afon — river
Allt — wooded hill or cliff
Aran — high place, mountain

Bach — small, corner
Bala — joining of lake to river
Banc — bank, hill
Bedd — grave
Bont — bridge
Bron — breast of hill or slope
Bryn — hill
Bwlch — pass or col
Bychan — small

Cadair — seat, strong-hold
Cae — field
Caer — fort
Capel — chapel
Carn — cairn
Carreg — stone
Carrog — stream
Cefn — ridge
Celli — grove
Clogwyn — cliff, precipice
Clwyd — gate
Coed — trees
Craig — rock
Crib — ridge
Croes — cross, crossroads

Din, Dinas — fort
Dre — homestead

Drws — door, pass
Du, Ddu — black
Dwy — two
Dyffryn — valley

Eglwys — church
Erw — acre
Esgair — long ridge

Fach — small
Fawr — large, great, extensive
Fechan — small
Ffair — fair
Fford — road
Ffraw — rapid
Ffrith — meadow
Foel — bare hill
Fychan — small

Garth — hill
Glan — brink, edge
Glas — blue, green
Glyder — sheltered valley
Glyn — valley
Gwydd — trees
Gwyddfa — wild place
Gwynt — wind

Hafod — summer home
Hen — old
Hendre — winter home
Hyll — ugly

Isaf — lower

Llain — stretch of land
Llan — church or enclosed
   space
Llanerch — clearing glade
Llech — stone slab
Llety — small house
Llyn — lake

Maen — stone
Maes — field
Mam — mother
Mawr — great, extensive
Melin — mill
Merch (plural Merchedd) —
   woman
Moel — bare or rounded
   mountain
Morfa — coastal marsh
Mynydd — mountain

Nant — brook, valley
Neuadd — hall
Newydd — new
Nos — night

Ogof — cave

Penrhyn — headland
Pant — hollow ground
Parc — field

Penmaen — rocky headland
Pennant — head of valley
Pentre — village, hamlet
Pig — summit
Pistyll — cataract
Plas — hall
Pont — bridge
Porth — harbour, bay

Rhos — moorland
Rhyd — ford

Saeth — arrow
Sarn — causeway

Tal — front
Tan — below
Traeth — beach
Tyn — small farm
Tywyn — shore

Uchaf — upper

Wen — white

Y — the
Yr — the
Ynys — island
Ysbyty — hospital
Ystryd — street

2

CLWYD
— AFON DEE AND THE
BORDER AREA

Approaching the county of Clwyd across the plains of Shropshire or Cheshire, the hills can be seen ahead for many miles. They sit dark and sombre along the horizon. Then almost immediately you cross the border you are amongst them, either climbing steeply or winding along deep valleys. The contrast between the landscapes of England and Wales is sometimes surprising.

The Clwydian hills, stretching from the northern coast down to Llangollen and with the Berwyns to the south, form a natural boundary which in years gone by must have been formidable for travellers and invaders. They are in general comfortable hills, pleasing to the eye and pleasant, on a fine day, to stroll amongst.

The Afon Dee, one of the major rivers of Wales, bisects these great ranges and winds through Llangollen, round far to the east of Wrexham and through the old city of Chester, *Deva* to the Romans, finally emerging to the sea at Flint to form the northern seaboard. There are few visitors to North Wales who will not cross it somewhere on their journey.

The eastern foothills which follow the curve of the Dee are composed mainly of coal measures with an underlying bed of limestone that comes to the surface occasionally as the scarp edges south of Maeshafn and on the Eglwyseg Mountains above Llangollen. It was probably the limestone deposits and the minerals

PLACES TO VISIT
IN AND NEAR WREXHAM

Erddig Hall
1 mile south of Wrexham off A438.
Late seventeenth- and early eighteenth-century mansion, features include outbuildings, domestic offices and portraits of staff. Original furniture in main rooms. Large gardens and parkland with Visitor Centre. National Trust Property.

St Giles Church
Wrexham
Fine wrought iron gates dating from 1720. Decorated steeple, some interesting contents within church. Grave of Elihu Yale, benefactor of Yale University.

Wrexham-Maelor Library and Art Centre
Rhosddu Road, Wrexham
Has visiting exhibitions from England and Wales.

Bersham Industrial Centre
2 miles south-west of Wrexham. Industrial archaeology museum relating to iron and coal. Leaflet available.

Milestone Visitor Centre
Bwlchgwyn, on A525 Wrexham-Ruthin Road.
Geological Museum of Wales, housing relics of distant and recent past. Folk displays and trails.

in these hills, particularly lead ores, which brought the first industry to the area. It is known that the Romans mined lead here using local labour, but it was not until the sixteenth and seventeenth centuries, when lead became such an important commodity, that the industry really developed. The most important use for lead was the lining of the roofs of houses and churches. During the heyday of the lead industry money was invested heavily in mining in these limestone hills. The mines stretch from Halkyn Mountain near Prestatyn in the north to Minera west of Wrexham. Massive beam engines were brought up from Cornwall to pump the mines clear of water, but it is only the overgrown square stone remains of the engine houses and their chimneys with the surrounding waste tips which survive as reminders of a once-thriving industry.

Iron ore mined in the hills and coal fields surrounding Wrexham led to the establishment in the eighteenth century of a thriving

Horse-powered mine winding engine at the Bersham Industrial Museum

smelting industry with iron works in Bersham, Ruabon and Wrexham. Other local resources, including clay for bricks and tiles, zinc ores and wool from the local sheep, soon made this area the most industrialised and populous in North Wales. Bersham was the main supplier of cannons to the British army during the Peninsular War. The iron ore eventually ran out and the Wrexham-based industry was moved north to a site near Queensferry on the Afon Dee to allow direct imports of the raw materials by sea. During 1980, however, under Government rationalisation plans for the steel industry, this major employer on Deeside finally closed its doors.

Wrexham (Wrecsam) and its environs now support a few industries, but most of those based on local resources have declined, leaving their remains for the industrial archaeologist to explore. This area of Wales is now designated as a development area by the government, and industries large and small are encouraged to move here to provide much-needed employment.

In the centre of Wrexham stands the church of St Giles, notable for its decorated tower built in 1506 and surmounted by four graceful hexagonal turrets. To the west of the tower is the grave of Elihu

The bridge and church at Bangor-on-Dee

Yale, the main benefactor of Yale University in America. It was restored by the members of the university in 1968 to mark the 250th anniversary of this benefaction. A replica of the tower of the church stands at Yale.

Virtually on the outskirts of Wrexham is Bersham, where John Wilkinson the famous eighteenth-century ironmaster made the cylinders for James Watt's steam engines and made cannons. The cannon boring mill and remains of the furnaces still survive, but are still being excavated and conserved so are not open for visitors. An industrial museum in the village concentrates on displays of the iron and coal industries.

To the east of Wrexham is an area known as Wrexham Maelor, which projects into the plains of Cheshire and Shropshire. The district was originally known as Maelor Saesneg (Saxon Maelor) and was established by Edward I as a detached part of Flint. Its character is more English than Welsh, as are many of the village names, but it has firmly remained part of Wales through the centuries, despite its vulnerable position. It finally lost its identity, and became part of Clwyd in the early 1970s. An important crossing

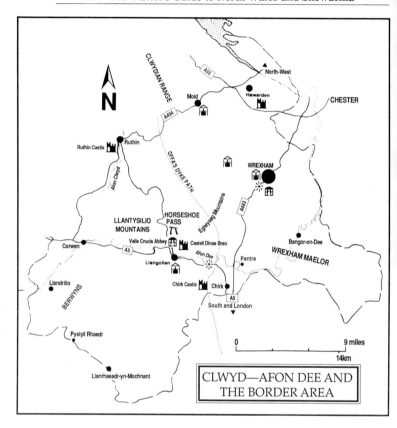

CLWYD—AFON DEE AND
THE BORDER AREA

point for the River Dee in this area was at Bangor-on-Dee (Bangor-is-y-coed), with its attractive old stone bridge and church. This small village was the site of the first monastery founded on British soil about AD180. The monastery was destroyed in AD607 by Ethelfrid of Northumbria, when 1,200 monks were slain. The few survivors are said to have established the first religious community on Bardsey Island. The main Wrexham to Whitchurch road now bypasses the village.

About one mile south of Wrexham and standing in a large estate, is the mansion of Erddig Hall, which was started in 1684 and finally completed about 1721-4 by John Meller, a London lawyer. With his nephew Simon Yorke he collected much of the fine silver and gilt furniture that can be seen here today. The property passed to Simon in 1733 and remained in the Yorke family until given to the National Trust in 1973. The family had always been good to their staff and the servants' hall has many portraits of particularly favourite staff. Visitors now enter through the stables and laundry, which, along with the restored sawmill, smithy and bakehouse, give a good idea of the domestic arrangements of an eighteenth-century house. There is a formal walled garden with old varieties of fruit trees, a dovecote complete with doves, extensive woods and parkland and a visitor centre.

Despite being the most industrial and extensively populated area of North Wales this corner of Clwyd has remained only a narrow strip. The nearby countryside is always accessible and only a short journey is necessary to leave all behind and reach the hills and valleys around **Llangollen**.

Here is a town so typically Welsh from its greystone houses to its wooded hillsides that it is hard to believe that one is only a few miles from the English border. One needs go no further than Llangollen to experience much of what Wales has to offer, and it has justifiably been a popular tourist centre for many years. George Borrow started his epic Welsh journey here in 1854 by describing Llangollen in his book *Wild Wales* as 'a small town or large village'. The town sits on both sides of the Afon Dee: the centre, with shops, cafés and hotels on the south bank of the river, is connected by a stone bridge to the thin strip of houses squeezed between the canal and the main road on the north of the river. The bridge was built originally in 1345, but it has been strengthened and improved through the centuries to cope with the increasing volume of traffic which frequently causes quite a bottleneck on a sunny summer's day. Upstream of the town is a suspension bridge for pedestrians, known as the Chain Bridge.

The town is perhaps best known for the International Musical Eisteddfod which is held to the east of the town in July every year. It attracts singers, musicians and dancers from all over the world. The town comes alive with national costumes and a true spirit of international friendship during these weeks.

The walled garden at Erddig on an Edwardian day.
Inset: *The main front*

PLACES TO VISIT
IN AND NEAR LLANGOLLEN

Chwarel Wynne Slate Mine and Museum
Glyn Ceiriog, 4 miles on scenic mountain road south of Llangollen.
Slate mine to visit, craft shop and picnic spot with nature trails.

Llangollen Motor Museum
Pentrefelin.
Collection of yesteryear's cars.

Pontcysyllte Aqueduct
Carries canal 120ft above Afon Dee, 1,000ft long. Superb position. Off Wrexham Road.

Plas Newydd
House of 'Ladies of Llangollen', beautiful black and white house in lovely gardens. South of river, well signposted.

Castell Dinas Bran
Thirteenth-century hilltop castle. Dominates the valley. Walk signposted from canal bridge on north side of river.

Canal Exhibition Centre
Llangollen.
Models and films tell the story of growth and use of canals. Horse drawn boat trips. On canal just across road from main bridge.

Llangollen Railway Society
Railway Station, Llangollen.
Passenger trains now operate to

Berwyn on the former Great Western Railway's Ruabon-Barmouth line. A varied collection of rolling stock and locomotives in the station and goods yard. By bridge across the river.

Valle Crucis Abbey
1½ miles north of Llangollen on A542 to Ruthin.
Substantial remains in a fine setting.

Eliseg's Pillar
1,000-year-old pillar tells story of Eliseg, ½ mile up valley from Valle Crucis Abbey.

Horseshoe Pass
On A542 Ruthin Road, 5 miles north of Llangollen.
Steep climb with good views, acquired by National Trust.

Horseshoe Falls
On Afon Dee 1 mile east of town centre. Built by Telford to provide water for canal system.

Chirk Castle
½mile west of Chirk village. Large fortress partially converted to stately home. Fine furniture, tapestries and portraits. Formal gardens with clipped yews and flowering shrubs. Owned by National Trust.

Canoeing below the bridge in Llangollen

Half a mile from the town centre is the old house of Plas Newydd (not to be confused with the National Trust house of the same name on Anglesey, overlooking the Menai Strait), once the house of two eccentric old ladies known throughout the country as the 'Ladies of Llangollen'. The ladies, the Hon Miss Sarah Ponsonby and Lady Eleanor Butler, resided at the house from 1779 until their deaths in 1829 and 1831. They were known for their rather eccentric style of dress and for the variety of their visitors — Wellington, Sir Walter Scott, who later immortalised the house in *The Betrothed*, and Wordsworth, all of whom were expected to contribute to the ladies' collection of old oak curios. Wordsworth's contribution was a rather

Plas Newydd, Llangollen

The Chain Bridge over the Afon Dee, near Llangollen

disdainful sonnet, which was not liked by the ladies — he was not invited back.

There is not much room between the river and the steeply rising hills to the north, but in that short space is squeezed a railway station, now home of the Llangollen Railway Society, a busy main road and a canal. In this limited area it is possible to study transport through the ages, for just above the station is the Canal Exhibition Centre on a spur of the Shropshire Union Canal. This is appropriate as the Llangollen Branch was one of the earliest of Britain's derelict waterways to be restored for leisure cruising. Running from Hurleston Junction on the Shropshire Union Canal it passes through beautiful countryside on its way to Llangollen.

Climbing steeply from just opposite the canal bridge is a footpath to Castell Dinas Bran, a stone castle perched 1,000ft above the town. Originally the site of an Iron Age hillfort, it later became a Norman stronghold and, finally, a little-used stone castle built in 1236 which had become a ruin by 1578. The climber is rewarded by a fine view — the long limestone escarpment of

A lifting bridge, typical of those on the Llangollen Canal

The canal basin at Trevor

The Pontcysyllte Aqueduct

Chirk Castle

Eglwyseg Rocks and the valleys radiating to the west and the north of the town. It is a magnificent place for a castle.

A narrow road rises steeply from the bridge and runs up the valley below Eglwyseg Mountain to the ford at World's End. There is parking space below the ford and a short walk can be taken along the gorge onto the moorland and forests above. If you continue along the road it takes you out onto the open moorland, mainly sheep grazing land, before finally descending to the old lead mining community of Minera.

The Afon Dee is at its wildest above Llangollen as it descends rapidly from just below the Horseshoe Falls in a series of small cataracts that tumble between the narrow banks — the venue of an annual canoe race. The Horseshoe Falls were built by Thomas Telford, the famous road and canal engineer, in 1806, to feed water into a spur of the Shropshire Union Canal running alongside and above the river before crossing 127ft above the river on the 1,000ft-long Pontcysyllte Aqueduct three miles down river from Llangollen. The aqueduct is a marvellous engineering achievement, as it

Detail of the gates at Chirk Castle

carries the canal in an iron trough supported on eighteen tall, slim stone pillars. The visitor with a head for heights can walk along the towpath across the viaduct from either the canal basin at Trevor at the northern end, or park in a small car park at Fron Cysyllte at the other end and cross the canal by one of the waterway's character-istic lifting bridges. Perhaps the most impressive view of the aqueduct is not from the top, but from below. A recently improved path down to the Afon Dee starts from the Trevor canal basin and to look up at the stone pillars soaring above one's head makes it obvious why this was regarded almost as a miracle when it was first built, and as one of the wonders of the Industrial Revolution.

Travellers from the south will miss Wrexham altogether and enter Wales close to the small border town of Chirk. To the west of the Telford A5 trunk road they will see an adjacent aqueduct and viaduct spanning the Ceiriog valley. The former carries the Shrop-shire Union Canal, and was built by Telford in 1801; the latter was built in 1848 to carry the railway.

Chirk owes its origins to an eleventh-century castle built origi-

The Vale of Llangollen

nally on the motte close to the church. This small Norman castle was superseded in the thirteenth century by a substantial stone castle built two miles away by Edward I to protect the English/Welsh Border or 'Marches'. Chirk Castle, now owned by the National Trust, is the only Marcher castle to have been occupied continuously since it was built. For the visitor it has the contrast of a medieval castle with towers, courtyard, steep narrow stairs, bare cold guard-rooms and a deep forbidding dungeon, with richly-appointed Adam-style staterooms. The beautiful formal gardens include notable topiary yew hedges and many flowering shrubs which are especially fine in springtime. A pair of magnificent wrought iron gates, made at Bersham in 1721, which once stood near the castle, now stand guard at the entrance to the $1^1/_2$-mile long drive.

The A5 trunk road, one of Telford's wonders, stretches from London to Holyhead and has been for more than a century and a half the main access to North Wales from England and the south. Running along the bottom of the Vale of Llangollen it provides many of the best views of the river and the surrounding hills. On the north side, the hills lean away from the road and are heather-clad in summer, but to the south the hills are heavily afforested and seem to become more so every year. Rising steeply from the very back of Llangollen the road to Llanarmon Glyn Ceiriog and Llanarmon Dyffryn-Ceiriog takes one into some of the most beautiful country-side in North Wales. The narrow lanes meander steeply up and down the deep valleys as forests and hills vie for attention. Such a large area of Wales seems seldom to be visited and it has none of the trappings associated with tourism. It is crossed by only one road — fortunately an ancient trackway unusable by anything but four-wheel drive vehicles — but what a splendid route it is, going right over the ridge between Llanarmon Dyffryn-Ceiriog and Llandrillo, crossing the pass below Cadair Bronwen.

These hills, the **Berwyns**, provide some of the best walking for many miles and can be recommended for experienced walkers as one of the quietest and least frequented parts of North Wales, but one of the most easily accessible. The long ridge walk from Moel Fferna in the north, over the Berwyns to Moel Sych in the south is well worthwhile, but a map and compass will be essential.

Much of this countryside was explored by the intrepid George

Pistyll Rhaeadr, the highest waterfall in Wales

Borrow in the 1850s, as he walked many of the lanes and visited many of the villages. One of the towns he describes with little enthusiasm is **Llanrhaeadr-yn-Mochnant**, home of Bishop William Morgan who made the first translation of the Bible into Welsh during the reign of Elizabeth I. Upstream from the village at the head of a steep sided valley is Pistyll Rhaeadr, the highest waterfall in Wales. Now largely surrounded by trees, it is difficult to appreciate the 240ft cascade from a distance. There is however a small car park by a quaint old farmhouse at the end of the lane and after a short walk one can see the full height from a bridge over the stream.

Valle Crucis Abbey

M
1-5h
**
††

The more intrepid walker can continue to the top of the falls by a steep footpath, starting from a grey gate opposite the farm, which zig zags up one side to the top, though this is a rather airy viewpoint. A walk upstream takes one into some fine country — the hills are wild, the ridge walks superb and the scenery splendid: but paths are rare, so go prepared.

To the west, the Berwyns drop slowly down to the Afon Dee as it casually meanders through the farming and forestry communities of Llandrillo and Cynwyd. Above **Llandrillo** on the slopes of Cadair Bronwen is a stone circle about 40ft in diameter. What its purpose and origin was we shall probably never know, but whoever placed it there chose the spot well for the views of the hills and the valley and the feeling of spaciousness are outstanding. It was an ideal place for religious meetings, if that was its purpose.

Joining the Afon Alwen, the Afon Dee turns east towards Llangollen, passing the market town of **Corwen** on its way. To the north the Llantysilio Mountains above Corwen are crowned by the Iron Age fort of Caer Drewyn. The heather-clad slopes run north-east to the top of the Horseshoe Pass, where the remains of the once thriving slate industry scar the landscape.

About two miles to the north-east of Llangollen on the road to Ruthin before it crosses the Horseshoe Pass, is Valle Crucis Abbey, beautifully situated in the centre of what must have been an idyllic valley. The extensive ruins of the church and some of the domestic buildings, now almost surrounded by a caravan site, give an idea of the abbey's former size. It was founded by Madog ap Gruffyd in 1201 for the Cistercian Order, dissolved in 1535, and now stands to remind us of its former beauty.

The abbey is believed to have taken its name from the pillar standing about $1/_2$ mile to the north, Eliseg's Pillar, which stands on a mound. Now well worn, it was carved with a Latin inscription in memory of Eliseg who reclaimed Powys (now Clwyd) from the English in the eighth century. Perhaps Eliseg is buried under the mound.

The mountains are crossed here by the main Llangollen to Ruthin road by way of the famous Horseshoe Pass, where the road climbs around a cirque. It is justifiably popular and there is a
 viewpoint at the head of the pass looking down towards Valle Crucis

PLACES OF INTEREST IN AND AROUND RUTHIN

Ruthin Castle
Norman castle with chequered history. Now a ruin and incorporated into an hotel.

Court House
Stands in main square. Lovely black and white building, was old prison with gallows, now a bank.

Exmewe Hall
Opposite Court House. Built about 1500 by Thomas Exmewe, Lord Mayor of London. Now a bank.

Maen Huail
Large stone in front of Exmewe Hall on which King Arthur is reputed to have behead Huail, his rival in love.

Church of St Peter
North-east corner of square. Fourteenth century with magnificent panelled ceiling given to the men of Wales by Henry VII.

Ruthin Craft Centre
Exhibition and workshops of many different crafts, which are worth seeing.

Abbey and Llangollen. As the friendly sheep always seem to be hungry, car doors should be kept firmly closed. The Llantysilio Mountains, which the road crosses, continue eastwards to the Eglwyseg Mountains, which curve round to the Llandegla Moors to join the Clwydian Range, which eventually terminates in the limestone quarries above Prestatyn on the north coast.

Offa's Dyke follows the line of these hills. Constructed about AD748 and running from Chepstow in South Wales, it follows roughly the present border until it crosses the Afon Dee downstream from Llangollen, before climbing up and over Eglwyseg Mountain to World's End and then heads north-west along the hills to Prestatyn. It is now a designated long distance footpath of 167 miles and, though a shadow of its former self, can still be seen in several parts of these hills. At one time its massive earth work was 20ft wide, with a bank on one side 12ft high, and was probably designed more as a deterrent than an effective barrier, though the actual hills themselves must have been a daunting prospect. Wales is probably more Welsh to the west of it than to the east, and it is on

The Old Court House (left) and Exmewe Hall (right), Ruthin

the western side that the Welsh-speaking parts generally lie.

The main road (A494) from Chester to Corwen is one of the main access routes to North Wales and cuts across this range of hills from Mold through Loggerheads, a popular area for short walks, before crossing the shoulder of Moel Famau and dropping into the Vale of Clwyd at Ruthin.

Ruthin or Rudd-Din — meaning red fortress — is built on a small hill above the Afon Clwyd. It is notable for the remains of the castle, built above a red sandstone cliff near the centre of the town. The town probably grew around the castle, which was strategically placed to watch over the river and the road which even in those days was one of the main routes from England. The original Welsh castle built by Prince Llewelyn's brother, Dafydd, was taken by Edward I in 1282 during the Welsh uprising and remained in English hands until dismantled as a Royalist stronghold by General Mytton in 1647 during the Civil War. Ruthin Castle now houses a luxury hotel.

A recently built bypass has eased the congestion in the narrow streets and open square of the town centre. Two banks occupy the notable buildings on the main square. To the south a fine old black and white building is the former Court House dating from 1401, which served as both prison and courthouse. A short beam, which was once the gallows, still projects below the eaves. On the west side is the sixteenth-century Exmewe Hall in front of which is the Maen Huail, a stone on which King Arthur is said to have beheaded Huail, his rival in love. The hall was built by Thomas Exmewe, who later became Lord Mayor of London.

The church of St Peter stands to the north-east of the square. At one time it was a collegiate church, and dates in parts from the thirteenth and fourteenth centuries. The interior has a magnificent oak panelled roof, made of 500 carved panels, every one different, which was presented to all the men of Wales by Henry VII for their help in gaining the throne for him.

The remains of Iron Age hillforts and barrows on the hilltops around the town show signs of earlier habitation. The hills here are certainly more friendly than those further west in Snowdonia: perhaps this attracted the old tribes. Today they are crossed by many roads, from which many walks can be enjoyed along the good network of footpaths, with an Ordnance Survey map.

3
CLWYD —
THE COAST AND INLAND

Clwyd was formed in 1974 during local government re-organisation as an amalgamation of the two counties of Flintshire and Denbighshire and is part of the old Welsh region of Gwynedd. It takes its most recent name from the Afon Clwyd which bisects the county, and is bounded on its eastern side by England and the Afon Dee, while its western boundary runs a few miles east of the Afon Conwy. For this chapter a more logical boundary is the Afon Conwy. The area has two main attractions for the visitor: the inland hills for walkers and sightseers, and the beautiful beaches on the northern coast for those who like a more relaxing day.

The coastlands are flat: there is a choice of roads from Queensferry, either the inland route, the A55 which is mainly a dual carriageway, or the more scenic coast road the A548, giving easy access to all the resorts. On both routes there are many reminders of the area's turbulent history, particularly of Edward I's attempts to subdue the Welsh princes in the late thirteenth century, when he built castles at all strategic points to maintain law and order. There are many fine ruins from this 'ring of steel' for the visitor to enjoy, most of them only slightly off the beaten track.

After crossing the Afon Dee at Queensferry or Chester the coastal road runs through some of the most depressing scenery in the whole of the county, as it follows for many miles the culmination

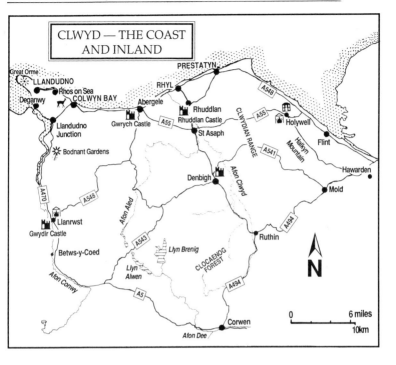

of hundreds of years of industrialisation. Though the estuary is never more than a mile away, it is only glimpsed occasionally between the mammoth buildings, many of which are now redundant. Fortunately this industrial zone is limited to a very narrow belt, backing on to the estuary, and can be easily avoided by using the inland route.

Inevitably, after conquering Wales, Edward I built a fortification on the first high ground after Chester. He chose the site of an Iron Age fort at **Hawarden** and there built a stone castle with a round tower. Some parts remain today, but much of it was destroyed by the Parliamentarians in 1646. A later house, started in 1750 and still standing below the castle, was the home of one of Queen Victoria's Prime Ministers, William Gladstone, who acquired the estate when he married Catherine Glynne. He lived there for sixty years and the

THINGS TO SEE ALONG DEESIDE

Hawarden Castle
Remains of Edward I's castle in grounds of William Gladstone's house. Close to village centre.

Ewloe Castle
Welsh castle built by Llewelyn the Last, to keep watch on Hawarden Castle. Two miles from Hawarden on A55.

Flint Castle
On edge of estuary with interesting defensive features including separate donjon. Off main square in town.

   neat little village bears many reminders of this most famous resident. There is a Gladstone museum, a commemorative window and an effigy in the church almost opposite the main gates to the estate, and a statue also near the gates. Next to the church in Hawarden is the Deiniol Library founded by Gladstone in 1895 and housing a collection of theological books and pamphlets which are available for study.

 Just two miles away from Edward's castle at Hawarden stand the remains of Ewloe Castle, now surrounded by trees and barely visible from the road. It was built by Llewelyn the Last about 1260 and is typical of a Welsh stone castle, built to provide a buffer between the warring English and Welsh.

It is difficult now to imagine the importance of this area in past times; it was the main route into Wales from Chester and England, for the hills further inland were inhospitable and dangerous to cross. The coastal belt was the main highway for all invading armies from the Romans onwards. As it is also easier to supply armies by sea than over land, the area has always been strategically important.

To complement the castle at Hawarden which guarded the inland route, Edward I built a fortress at **Flint** to protect the coastal route and the estuary of the Afon Dee. The castle, built on rock on the very edge of the sands, is all that remains of a once walled town. It is just off the main square and missed by the many visitors who head each year for the beaches further along the coast. One tower

The ruins of Flint Castle

is detached from the main body of the castle and is connected by a drawbridge; it is the only example of this in the country. The tower or donjon was to be the last line of defence. The castle was the scene of the betrayal of Richard II and was immortalised in Shakespeare's play, much of which is set there. Today the castle is almost surrounded by buildings, and the Dee continues to silt up. The port that flourished until the last century no longer exists and today the town relies on modern industry for its survival.

The new county town is **Mold**, just five miles to the south of Flint. Unlike its predecessor it occupies a position of no particular geographical or historical importance, though it is a very pleasant little town. There was a small Norman castle on Bailey Hill at one end of the High Street, and the church, which is fifteenth century, has some fine stained glass windows and friezes carved with animals.

Mold was the home in the nineteeth century of Daniel Owen, a novelist and short story writer, who wrote in the Welsh language about Welsh people. He was a tailor who spent most of his life in the

PLACES TO VISIT
IN MOLD

Daniel Owen Centre
Early Road, Mold
Exhibition centre of local arts
and memorial museum to Daniel
Owen, one of Wales' leading
novelists.

Theatr Clwyd
Three theatres under one roof,
regular programme of films,
concerts and live exhibitions.
Has its own professional
company. Close to town centre.

 town. There is now a small museum at the Daniel Owen Centre containing memorabilia of this fine author.

Each Saturday, the main street in Mold is closed for the market, the stalls of which are set up on each side of the road. Perhaps of less interest to the visitor but more noticeable by their size are the new administrative buildings of Clwyd County Council which are about half a mile from the town centre on the Chester road. There too is the Theatr Clwyd, a centre for entertainment and arts. There are regular concerts, and the theatre has its own professional company.

L
1-1½h
*
††

On the opposite side of the town the A494 Ruthin road rises steeply to the Rainbow Inn, before dropping even more steeply down to the Loggerheads Inn at the bottom of a deeply wooded valley. There is a car park here and short walks can be taken along the valley and through the woods — a pleasant spot to spend an afternoon. There are some steep limestone cliffs above the woods which give a feeling of depth to this little valley.

M
1-2h
*
†††

Continuing along the main Ruthin road a minor road, probably the original road, turns off to the right about one mile after Loggerheads. If one takes this to the top of the pass and parks for a short while there are some breathtaking views over Ruthin and the Vale of Clwyd to the north and the sea. From the parking spot there is a good footpath leading up to the Jubilee Tower on the summit of Moel Famau. The tower was built to commemorate George III's jubilee. It is now part of a country park and on a clear day one can sometimes see the Isle of Man and the mountains of the Lake District to the north; but the closer views of Snowdonia to the west

THINGS TO SEE IN AND AROUND HOLYWELL

St Winifride's Chapel
Holywell
Built by Margaret Beaufort,
mother of Henry VII, it houses
the Holy Well. A destination for
pilgrims for centuries.

Basingwerk Abbey
Off A548, 1 mile north of
Holywell
Praised for its beauty and
setting. Ruins fairly extensive.

Military Museum
Off the A55, $^3/_4$ mile west of
Holywell
Housed in an underground
cavern is a large collection of
military vehicles, weapons and
medals. Picnic area and café.

Maen Achwyfan
Whitford, 4 miles north-west of
Holywell
Eleventh-century carved Celtic
cross.

are more rewarding. It is a pleasant stroll, well worth doing. From the car park the single track road descends steeply into Ruthin and requires care.

To the north of Mold is Halkyn Mountain which runs nearly parallel with the estuary. It is composed mainly of limestone and for many centuries was the source of much of the wealth of the county; it was riddled with lead and lead mines. There are many remains of engine houses and tunnels of interest to the industrial archaeologist. The Romans mined here but it was the nineteenth-century entrepreneurs who used their technology to sink even deeper mines and longer tunnels. Water seepage was always a serious problem and it was not until 1878 that a tunnel almost the full length of the mountain drained the mines into the estuary.

Today the hill is extensively quarried for limestone, but for walkers there are excellent views across the Dee estuary, the Wirral and the Mersey estuary to Liverpool and the Lancashire plain.

On the northern slopes of Halkyn Mountain stands the small town of **Holywell**, once a centre for many pilgrims. The well is said to have curative powers and is part of St Winifride's Chapel, a church built in perpendicular style by Margaret Beaufort, the mother of Henry VII. Pilgrims enter the bath by steps, and kneel to pray on

St Winifride's Chapel, Holywell

the stone of St Beuno, founder of an earlier chapel on the site. The Holy Well was originally fed by a spring from the nearby limestone hills, but since the early part of this century has been fed by a small reservoir. Until the Reformation, the well was in the care of the Cistercian monks from nearby Basingwerk Abbey. The abbey, just a mile north-east of Holywell in a beautiful setting, was known for its fine building and windows. It was taken apart at the Dissolution and the present remains, which are mainly thirteenth century (though the original abbey was founded in 1132), give some idea of the extent of the building.

North-west of Holywell, near Whitford, is Maen Achwfan, an impressive early eleventh-century stone cross elaborately carved

Maen Achwfan, near Whitford, close to Holywell

with Celtic designs. Standing 11ft high it is the tallest of its type in Britain. It is signposted from the nearby village.

Modern visitors in the summer will be content to bypass the towns backing the Dee Estuary and speed west along the coast to the seaside towns and caravan sites which for many are the attractions in this part of Wales. From the colliery at the Point of Ayr the fields bordering the coastal road become a continuous mass of caravan sites and holiday camps which from Easter onwards attract visitors from all over Britain. It is a popular area for family holidays and weekend visitors, as there are many fine beaches along this northern coast which are safe for bathing and boating.

Prestatyn, the first major town to be reached, is a pleasant place with three main beaches and two large holiday camps. Ffrith beach, the most northerly, has convenient parking, a play area with motor boats, a mini-golf course and other amusements. Central

BEACHES IN PRESTATYN AND RHYL

Ffrith Beach
Prestatyn
Motor boats, children's play area, donkey rides and other attractions.

Central Beach
Prestatyn
Open-air heated swimming pool. Royal Lido Centre with bars, cafés and shops.

Barkby Beach
Prestatyn
Good for launching boats, quieter than other beaches.

Rhyl Beach
Three miles of sandy beach, backed by a promenade. Cafés, children's playground, donkey rides, cinemas and all the fun of the fair. *Bathing is not advised on the western end near the mouth of the Afon Clwyd.*

Sun Centre
On promenade, Rhyl
Super modern swimming pools, with wave-making machine, café etc, all in glass-sided building.

Ocean Beach Park and Marine Lake
West end of promenade, Rhyl. Swings and roundabouts and all the fun of the fair.

beach has the Nova Centre backing onto it, a heated swimming pool if the sea is too cold, band concerts and bars. Barkby beach is perhaps a little quieter and has access for boat trailers. Central and Ffrith beaches are the best for bathing.

The town itself is a thriving community all the year round with many residents, and does not rely solely on summer visitors for its livelihood. There is a good range of shops, cafés and hotels. Inland from the coast is Meliden. Above Meliden is a range of limestone hills with several short walks which give excellent views all along the coast. Above Prestatyn on the road out to Gwaenysgor, there is a small car park before the road climbs steeply; the signpost shows the route to Offa's Dyke Path and a walk through the woods up to the top of the hills. This is the northern end of the Offa's Dyke Path mentioned in the previous chapter. Crowning the hill are the embankments of an old Iron Age fort. Just to the south at Gop Hill

Gwrych Castle, Abergele

are some caves where remains of Stone Age man have been found. For the archaeologist this area is particularly fascinating, for there is much evidence of prehistoric man.

Rhyl is only four miles from Prestatyn, but it seems much more on a busy Sunday when the traffic moves slowly. Perhaps the most famous seaside town in North Wales, catering for many thousands of visitors each year, it differs completely from its near neighbour and is so much more brash. There is something for everybody with all the necessary seaside amusements on the promenade, and a beach which is excellent for swimming, though one must take care at the western end near the mouth of the Afon Clwyd. Most of the major attractions are along the sea front on the wide promenade. The Sun Centre dominates the Eastern Parade, a large modern structure mainly of glass containing restaurants, amusements, a swimming pool with a wave-making machine and other swimming pools.

Further along is the Floral Hall, well known for its magnificent

Colwyn Bay

opposite: *The Sun Centre, Rhyl*   *Llandudno and the Great Orme*

WHAT TO SEE AROUND ABERGELE

Abergele Beach
Pensarn
Pebble beach but sand exposed
as the tide recedes. Popular for
caravans.

Gwrych Castle
Mock castle built in beautiful setting. Fine furniture inside, with
jousting and miniature railway in
grounds. Just off A55, west of
Abergele.

displays of flowers, a paddling pool, bandstand, and the Ocean
beach park with its roundabouts and all-the-fun-of-the-fair. Alongside is the Marine Lake for boating.

The Afon Clwyd with its once-wide estuary and reclaimed
marshland effectively forms the western boundary of the town, but
the road continues parallel with the sea through the fields of
caravans to **Abergele**, just four miles further on. This small town,
with a busy livestock sale on Mondays, seems to be more Welsh
than its neighour; at the junction of several main roads, its narrow
streets are always busy. It is a market town and the old church close

to the town centre contains some interesting relics of the past, with
some fifteenth- and sixteenth-century glass and a dug-out chest.
The churchyard has two memorials to disasters which happened in
the neighbourhood, the shipwreck of the *Ocean Monarch* in 1848
and the crash of the Irish Mail train twenty years later.

Although situated about a mile from the seashore, Abergele,
now joined to Pensarn on the coast, with its pebbly beaches and
sandhills, is a pleasant town for a more relaxing day.

On the outskirts of the town are the long walks and great
gatehouse surrounding Gwrych Castle, set below wooded hills in a

large estate. It is an impressive site, though unfortunately a folly, for
the castle was built in 1815 by a wealthy tycoon. It is open to the
public and contains many antiques and fine furnishings. The
parklands contain an amusement centre which has a miniature
railway and holds jousting contests on summer afternoons. There
are several short walks in the surrounding woodlands.

PLACES TO VISIT AROUND COLWYN BAY

Colwyn Beach
A long curving beach, round the bay. Good sand and safe bathing, very popular.

Eirias Park
Boating, bowls, tennis, picnic spots.

Prince of Wales Theatre
Regular variety shows, bands and plays.

Welsh Mountain Zoo
Collection of animals and birds of prey with free flying displays daily (weather permitting). Off A55 by West End Shopping Centre.

Rhos-on-Sea
Extension of Colwyn Bay, with Harlequin Puppet Theatre, open-air swimming pool (heated), and St Trillo's church on the beach.

The main road, now a dual carriageway for much of its length, speeds up and over the headland to Penmaen-Rhos with its huge limestone quarries, and then drops steeply into the back of Colwyn Bay.

Before the descent there is a fine viewpoint beside the main road where the sweep of the bay around to the Little Orme can be seen. The whole shoreline has beautiful sandy beaches with a promenade running almost the full curve of the bay.

Colwyn Bay, with its neighbour **Rhos-on-Sea**, has mushroomed in recent years to become a major holiday resort. Besides all the usual attractions along the promenade, including a pier, it has much to offer and many places of interest. Eirias Park runs south from the promenade, with picnic areas, boating, bowls, tennis and a sports area. The nearby Prince of Wales Theatre has a busy summer season with a variety of shows, while in Rhos there is the Harlequin Puppet Theatre, an open-air swimming pool just off the promenade and a golf course.

A curiosity on the seashore at Rhos is the miniature church of St Trillo built over a small holy well. The chapel is only 11ft by 8ft and is probably the smallest in Wales. The Celtic saint is believed to

Bodnant Gardens

PLACES OF INTEREST IN AND AROUND LLANDUDNO

Beaches
North Shore: Good beach backed by promenade. Safe bathing, launch facilities and water skiing area.
West Shore: Shingle beach, sea goes out a long way at low tide, so bathing is only when tide is in.
Lews Carroll Memorial

Great Orme
Nature trails, tramway and cabin lift to summit. Dry ski slope.

Happy Valley
Park with playground, rock gardens and open-air theatre.

Pier
With theatre and landing stage.

Rapallo House
Ffan Bach Road
Museum and arts centre with exhibits of local and national interest.

Bodnant Gardens
Beautiful gardens and woodlands, some of the finest in Europe. Especially noted for its rhododendrons in the spring. Six miles south of Llandudno Junction off A470. Owned by the National Trust.

Felin Isaf
Llansantffraid, Glan Conwy. Seventeenth-century flour mill with original machinery and methods.

have lived here for many years and local people say fishermen and sailors prayed there before a journey. Services are now held outside, and the church is open daily.

On the outskirts of the town is the famous Welsh Mountain Zoo where a wide variety of birds and animals are kept in as near natural surroundings a possible. There are many birds of prey, and weather permitting, daily flying displays of eagles, falcons, etc. Behind Rhos on Sea is the small Bryn Euryn. Although almost surrounded by roads it is nevertheless a pleasant place to stroll and to enjoy the panoramic views over the towns and bay.

L
1h
*
††

The road climbs over the shoulder of the Little Orme and then descends to follow the promenade to **Llandudno**, sheltered on a neck of land by the massive bulk of the Great Orme. The town straddles the low-lying land with the main amusement centres on

Lewis Carroll Memorial, West Shore, Llandudno

ON THIS VERY SHORE
DURING HAPPY RAMBLES WITH
LITTLE ALICE LIDDELL
LEWIS CARROLL
WAS INSPIRED TO WRITE THAT
LITERARY TREASURE
'ALICE IN WONDERLAND'
WHICH HAS CHARMED CHILDREN
FOR GENERATIONS.

UNVEILED BY
THE RT. HON. D. LLOYD GEORGE O.M. M.P.
SEPT. 5TH 1933.

the north-facing coast and the quieter residential areas overlooking the estuary of the Afon Conwy. The town retains much of its Victorian grandeur and gives the impression of being more conservative than its neighbours.

The promenade follows the curve of the bay and has most of the usual amusements. At the foot of the Great Orme is the Pier Pavilion. Attached is a landing stage for steamers which offer trips around the bay, along the coast and even to the Isle of Man. There are several theatres in the town attracting first class variety acts during the summer months, and it is best to enquire locally for the current attractions. Happy Valley is a public park where everybody

Bridge over the Afon Conwy at Llanrwst

should be made to smile; it has playgrounds, rockpools and an open-air theatre. From the park a cabin lift leaves for the summit of the Great Orme. Llandudno is not only an amusement centre: it has many fine shops in the main street. Rapallo House about a mile from the town centre is a museum and art gallery with many displays relating to Welsh history.

On the other side of the town, the West Shore, overlooking the Conwy estuary and Snowdonia, is generally quieter. It was here that Charles Dodgson, better known as Lewis Carroll, spent several holidays at the house of Dean Liddell, whose daughter inspired the tales of *Alice in Wonderland*. A memorial portraying the White Rabbit from those tales was unveiled there in 1933 by Lloyd George.

The Great Orme dominates Llandudno and protects it from the prevailing westerly winds. A toll road (Marine Drive) encircles the headland, giving some fine views of the cliffs, caves and coast to the south. It is possible to reach the summit café (679ft) by car, foot, tramway or cabin lift. The latter two are a continuous daily service during the summer months. There are many minor antiquities on

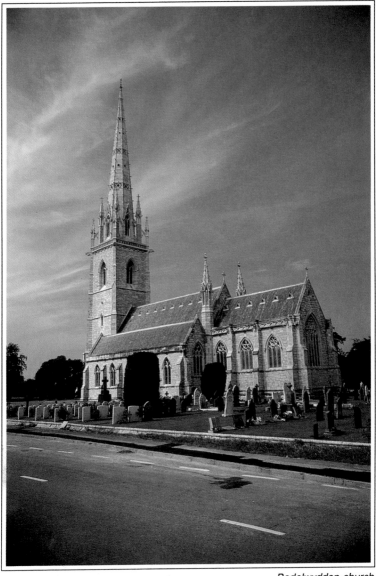

Bodelwyddan church

L
1-2h
*
†††

the hillsides and the Great Orme Nature Trail which starts in the Happy Valley is perhaps the best way to see them. It is also an excellent way of escaping from the hustle and bustle for a few hours and enjoying this magnificent setting.

A short distance to the south of Llandudno and standing on the shores of the Conwy estuary is **Deganwy**. With its castle, now only a ruin, it has for many centuries guarded the northern entrance to the Afon Conwy. Today, with a sheltered harbour, it is a popular resort and centre for sailing.

One of the best known attractions in this area is Bodnant Gardens, the home of Lord Aberconwy, five miles to the south of Deganwy. It is one of the finest gardens in Britain, well known for its wonderful collection of trees from all over the world. There are nearly a hundred acres of formal and informal gardens on the hillside overlooking the mountains of Snowdonia. In the spring there are magnificent displays of rhododendrons, azaleas, magnolias, camelias and a laburnum tunnel which is spectacular when it is in full flower. In the summer there are formal rose gardens and herbaceous borders.

The house here is not open to the public. The garden is laid in terraces down the side of the valley. Below the lawns surrounding the house is a large pond surrounded by mature trees and paths which lead down to a canal pond which features on many photographs of the gardens. Adjacent to this is the large area of woodland with magnificent rhododendrons. Below the wood in the bottom of the valley stands the estate watermill which Lord Aberconwy has just presented to the National Trust.

Up river from Bodnant, squeezed between the steep hills and the meandering river, is **Llanrwst**, a solid Welsh market town, It is a town little altered by tourism, that serves a wide community in the surrounding hills and forests. The Afon Conwy has many outstanding bridges, not least of which is the beautiful arched bridge here. Said to have been built by Inigo Jones in 1636, it was commissioned by the Wynn family who lived in Gwydir Castle on the opposite bank. There are other reminders of this wealthy family in the old church off the town square.

To the east of Llanrwst in the area bordered in the south by the inevitable A5 and in the north by the coast is a vast area of

PLACES TO VISIT IN AND AROUND LLANRWST

Gwydir Castle
Historic Tudor mansion, grounds with peacocks. Across the river from Llanrwst on B5106.

Trefriw Woollen Mills
Working woollen mill, showing all stages of the manufacture of tapestries and tweeds from the raw wool.

Gwydyr Forest
Extensive forests on west bank of river with many walks and nature trails. Leaflets available from Forestry Commission, Gwydyr Uchaf, Llanrwst.

North Wales Museum of Wild Life
On outskirts of town. It has a collection of game trophies and rare birds from round the world.

uncommercialised Wales. The hills to the north are gently rounded crossed by a zig-zag assortment of minor roads. There are lovely little villages and surprise views which for the car-bound visitor makes a pleasant interlude away from the bustling coastlands.

There are high moorlands with famous grouse shoots and hills that will give a good day's walking at a relatively low level. Much of the area has been afforested and once a year Clocaenog Forest echoes to screaming engines as competitors of the RAC rally tear down the forest roads on one of the many special stages through the Welsh forests.

In the centre of this area and signposted from most directions is Llyn Brenig, a reservoir opened by the Prince of Wales in 1976. Surrounding the reservoir and easily accessible for visitors is an area of unspoilt country. There are nature reserves and picnic areas around the lake and sailing and fishing on it. The information centre will provide details of the nature and history trails. It is perhaps one of the best areas in the country to look at prehistory. There is much evidence of early man with hut circles, burial mounds and enclo- sures dating from the Stone Age to more recent times. It is an area well worth exploring and within easy reach of the coastal resorts and close to a car park.

Rhuddlan Castle

PLACES OF INTEREST IN THE VALE OF CLWYD

Denbigh Castle and Leicester's Church
Interesting remains of important castle.

Llyn Brenig
6½ miles from Denbigh off B4501.
Reservoir for sailing, angling, pony trekking, has archaeological trail and visitors' centre.

St Asaph Cathedral
One of early churches of Wales, and smallest cathedral in Britain. Much added to over the years.

Chapter House. Museum with collection of religious papers.

Rhuddlan Castle
Solid looking castle on the edge of the Afon Clwyd. Historically important, but much damaged as source of local building materials.

Bodelwyddan
Near St Asaph
White 'marble' church, built in 1856. Can be seen for many miles around.

To the east is the historic former county town of **Denbigh** (known in Welsh as Dinbych), built a short distance above the river. The castle, built by Henry de Lacy in 1282 for Edward I to help maintain law and order in the region, changed hands frequently between the Welsh and the English. It was finally destroyed by the Roundheads in 1645 after an eleven-month siege; Charles I had taken refuge there after his defeat at Rowton Moor near Chester. It has a large and beautiful gatehouse and some interesting defensive ideas built in, though little now remains. Nearby are the walls of Leicester's church begun by the Earl of Leicester in 1579 to replace St Asaph's cathedral, but never completed. The remains of the town walls to the north of this ruin show how important Denbigh was in the past.

H. M. Stanley, the adventurer and the author of the remark 'Doctor Livingstone, I presume' was born in Denbigh, and Sir Hugh Myddleton, who constructed London's water supply in the reign of James I lived close by at Gwaunynog. Thomas Edwards a famous and well loved bard, and the author known as Twm o'r Nant, is buried in the parish church one mile east of the town.

Downstream from Denbigh is the cathedral town of **St Asaph**. Though the cathedral is perhaps less famous nowadays than the nearby white 'marble' church at Bodelwyddan it gives the place the status of a city, the smallest (as is the cathedral) in Great Britain. The cathedral is a squat building on the site of a church founded in AD560 by St Mungo, who was succeeded in AD573 by St Asaph, from whom the town takes its name. There has been a cathedral here ever since, despite Edward I's attempts to build an alternative at Rhuddlan. The present, much restored, building contains many features that have survived from earlier centuries. The Chapter Museum contains a fine collection of early religious manuscripts and Bibles, but it is open only by request and never on Sundays.

Three miles to the north is Rhuddlan Castle, perhaps one of the most solid-looking of all Edward's castles. It stands on the banks of the Clwyd, which was diverted and canalised to allow ships to sail in from the sea and berth at high tide. It guarded the main coastal route into North Wales and stands as a grim reminder to modern visitors of the troubled past of this land. Many people pass through **Rhuddlan** each year, but few realise that the valley to the south played such an important part in shaping the future of the Welsh people.

4

THE MOUNTAINS OF NORTHERN SNOWDONIA

Some visitors will perhaps explore only the resorts on the northern coast, but it is the mountains west of the Afon Conwy that are the attraction to many others. Rising steeply from the banks of the river, they are some of the highest peaks in England and Wales as well as some of the oldest. They are visible for many miles, and form a jagged skyline in sharp contrast to the surrounding moorlands.

For convenience the larger towns and villages will be visited first, for the hills are to a great extent the domain of the experienced climber and hillwalker, though there are several interesting excursions on foot for the novice. All the large towns are situated on the coast and events have shown how important the routes along the coastal belt have been in the past. To the modern traveller they are equally important, for they are the normal access routes for most people approaching from the north and north-west of England. After passing through Abergele both coastal roads become one busy main road (A55), threading through Colwyn Bay and Llandudno Junction to arrive at one of the main crossing points of the Afon Conwy.

There are three bridges across the Conwy estuary: Stephenson's tubular railway bridge, Telford's beautiful suspension bridge, which replaced an ancient and dangerous ferry and is now used

The Afon Conwy

only by pedestrians, and a modern road bridge which unfortunately has turned one of the most attractive historic towns in North Wales into a bottleneck for traffic during much of the summer. The suspension bridge, opened in 1826, was a major technical achievement of its time and was built by Thomas Telford, who was associated with many major transport projects in North Wales.

Work is progressing well on a road tunnel under the estuary which should be open in 1990. This will speed traffic along the coastal route and avoid Conwy town altogether. Visitors must divert off this route at Llandudno Junction to visit the town.

The town of **Conwy** is situated on the very edge of the estuary with the superbly sited castle dominating the town from its rocky perch above the river. It is one of the most interesting, and probably one of the most visited, towns in Wales. The walls surrounding the town are almost complete and with the castle form a unique defensive work. The enclosed narrow streets are as busy as the quay and landing stage. All contribute to make the town a popular holiday and yachting centre.

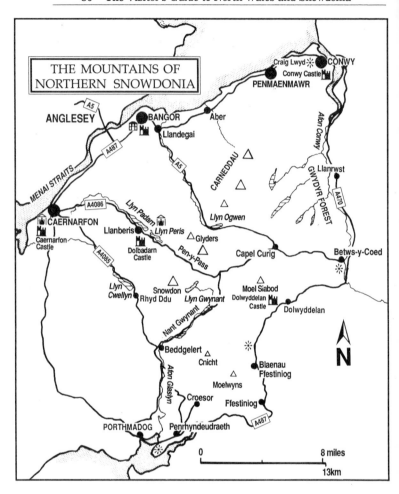

THE MOUNTAINS OF NORTHERN SNOWDONIA

The castle stands on the site of a Cistercian monastery built in the tenth century, but uprooted a hundred years later and moved to Maenan five miles upstream by Edward I, who saw the site as more suitable for defence than religion. The castle was built in only four years, a remarkable feat without modern mechanical aids, and served in part as a royal palace. During its stormy lifetime it has

The Smallest House, Conwy

regularly changed hands between the Welsh and English before finally being captured and dismantled by the Parliamentarians under General Mytton in 1646.

Modern visitors to the castle approach from Castle Square and it is from high on its walls that the best views of the nearby hills and the town walls can be seen. The walls were built at the same time as the castle and are part of an integral defensive scheme for the town; they follow the rise and fall of the land and are approximately 30ft tall with twenty-one towers throughout their length.

The quay is within the walls and has long been a port for fishing boats. Today it is becoming more important as a centre for yachts-

PLACES OF INTEREST IN AND AROUND CONWY

Plas Mawr
High Street, Conwy
Perfect example of Elizabethan building. Now houses Royal Cambrian Academy of Art.

Conwy Castle and Walls
Magnificent setting, best example in country.

Aberconwy House
Castle Street, Conwy
A good example of a fourteenth-century timber framed house. Houses Conwy Exhibition, depicting life of the town from Roman Times. Owned by National Trust.

St Mary's Church
Originally part of Cistercian Abbey but developed as a parish church over the years.

Smallest House
Britain's smallest house, on the quayside.

Conwy Mountain
Hut circles and footpaths in most directions.

Sychnant Pass
Old road connecting Conwy and Penmaenmawr.

men and boating enthusiasts, the harbour providing a safe mooring. It is a busy place, full of hustle and bustle, though still a pleasant place to sit and watch the world go by. On the quayside is Britain's smallest house, a tiny half-up and half-down, built by a bachelor who obviously intended to remain so.

Plas Mawr, perhaps the most visited building after the castle, is a fine example of an Elizabethan house; just off the High Street, it has many interesting features both inside and outside. Several of the rooms have associations with Elizabeth I and the Lantern Room is reputed to be haunted. There are 365 windows and 52 doors in the house, coinciding with the days and weeks of the year, a symbolic feature that the Elizabethans were quite fond of. It is now an art gallery housing the annual exhibition of the Royal Cambrian Academy of Art.

Lower down the High Street, Aberconwy is a white timber and stone house owned by the National Trust. It is the only survivor of

Conwy Castle

the type of medieval merchant's town house built in the fifteenth and sixteenth centuries which formerly abounded in Conwy.

Almost surrounded by houses and streets stands St Mary's church which occupies the site of the early Cistercian abbey. Much of the exterior structure is part of the original abbey, but the centuries have seen many additions to both inside and outside, and it is now a good example of the development of a parish church through the years. The churchyard includes the grave of two childen who are celebrated in William Wordsworth's poem *We Are Seven*, which he wrote in 1798.

Behind the town are some good hill walks with clear paths, particularly over Conwy Mountain (only 808ft high) to the Iron Age hillfort of Caer Leion. The old road crossed the Sychnant Pass behind Conwy to the coast at **Penmaenmawr**, and the head of the pass is a good place to park before enjoying one of the many short (or long) walks on the nearby slopes.

The river and the lakes upstream from Conwy are the breeding grounds for salmon. Several local families are licensed to catch the fish as they swim upstream, using nets which must not be below a particular mesh size, ensuring that only the larger fish are caught.

The modern road westwards from Conwy hugs the coast through a series of tunnels to give a smooth, quick ride through Penmaenmawr to Bangor. The old road over Sychnant Pass had a formidable reputation and many travellers preferred to walk along the shoreline than cross the pass. Frequently the road was so bad that carriages had to be dismantled to get them over the worst parts.

The hills to the south of the old and new roads have many reminders of the prehistoric people who inhabited the area. Just above Penmaenmawr at Craig Lwyd was a stone axe factory. Using the tough granite, Stone Age man chipped and shaped it, both for his own use and for 'export'; axes from the site have been found all over Britain. There are many other prehistoric sites, some of which have been combined into a history trail from Penmaenmawr; leaflets are available in local shops.

L
1-2h
∗
†††

Modern man still finds the granite worth quarrying, the summit of Penmaenmawr, from which the town gets its name, being a major source of this material; the height of the hill is reduced annually.

Aber, a short distance further on, is a small village known for the waterfall in the hills above. One turns off the main road and parks at the car park at the end of the valley. A walk of about a mile up the valley leads to the most impressive falls, which have a vertical drop of about 120ft. To the west are the smaller cataracts of Afon Bach. The hills south of the falls are owned by the National Trust, and the mountains of the Carneddau are some of the wildest and highest in Snowdonia. Aber's car park is an ideal starting point for walks into these hills, but only experienced walkers, able to use a map and compass, should consider such an expedition.

The coast road continues south to join the A5 trunk road at **Llandegai**. This busy road from London to Holyhead was built by Thomas Telford in the early nineteenth century to speed the journey, and especially the Royal Mail, to and from Ireland. Opposite the junction is Penrhyn Castle and estate, now run by the National Trust. Until recently it was the home of the Pennant family who were the former owners of the Penrhyn Slate quarries in Bethesda. The house, which overlooks the Menai Straits, is a masterpiece of neo-Norman architecture and for obvious reasons slate has been used extensively both inside and outside.

PLACES OF INTEREST IN AND AROUND BANGOR

Penrhyn Castle
Just off the A55 north of Bangor. An elegant neo-Norman mansion on the edge of the Menai Straits; many slate artefacts in the building. Doll museum and industrial railway museum. Owned by National Trust.

Theatr Gwynedd
County centre for theatre and films with regular performances.

Bangor Cathedral
Thought to be the oldest in Britain, shows evidence of continuous development since sixth century.

Old Canonry
Bangor
Houses Museum of Welsh Antiquities, with collection of seventeenth-century furniture illustrating Welsh rural crafts. Prehistoric and Romano-British objects.

The style and ostentatious design of the building reflect the unlimited amount of money available to many nineteenth-century businessmen. Parts of the building now house a doll museum, and on the estate is an industrial railway museum with locomotives and rolling stock from the Penrhyn and other slate quarries. In the old days, most of the slate shipped from the quarries went from the quay on the estate, so that the owner and management could keep a close eye on the amount being sold and despatched.

Bangor, one of the five university towns of Wales, stands at the northern end of the Menai Straits, most of the town being squeezed between two low hills in a shallow valley. It is dominated by the buildings of the University College of North Wales which stand on the hill between the town and the Straits. The university is perhaps modern Bangor's main claim to fame, though in the past it has been a Celtic centre for Christianity; a bishopric was established here as long ago as AD546.

The cathedral is thought to be the oldest in Britain in continuous use. The building, though not remarkable, has seen continuous de- velopment since Norman times and, despite suffering much at the

Penrhyn Castle

hands of both Welsh and English aggressors, bears much evidence of the many phases of its development. Restoration was begun in 1866 under the care of Sir Gilbert Scott, who approached it with an eye to the past and was able to include much detail that had been destroyed in previous centuries. Nearby is the old Bishop's Palace, built mainly in the sixteenth century and now the town hall. Almost opposite is the Theatr Gwynedd, the centre for the performing arts in the county. The Museum of Welsh Antiquities, housed in the Old Canonry near the cathedral, contains exhibits from prehistoric, Roman and more recent times giving a good background to the development of the town, surrounding area and Wales generally. The city was a quiet religious centre until early last century. The opening of the two bridges across the Menai Straits in the first half of the

Port Dinorwig

nineteenth century resulted in increased traffic by road and rail through the town. With the arrival of the university college in 1883, Bangor finally became a municipality and busy commercial centre.

Visitors may prefer to follow the A5 trunk road out of Bangor to see the Menai Straits; there is a fine viewpoint above the suspension bridge. The Straits, which divide Anglesey from the mainland, vary between 200yd and a mile wide and are thirteen miles long. They have formed an almost inpenetrable barrier for most invaders. The bridges were constructed in the nineteenth century and will be detailed in a later chapter. They did for the first time provide a crossing that was safe and to an extent opened up Anglesey to the Victorian tourist.

After leaving the bridges behind the road south moves a little inland before passing above **Port Dinorwig**. In the heyday of the slate quarry a narrow gauge railway came down from Llanberis to load the waiting ships at this tiny port with cut slates. Neglected for many years it has taken on a new life and is now a popular centre for yachting and holidays.

PLACES OF INTEREST IN CAERNARFON

Caernarfon Castle
Finest of Edward's castles.
Polygonal towers with banded
masonry make it unique.

Town Walls
Circle inner part of town, part of
integral defensive system.

Segontium
Roman Fort on outskirts of town.
Some buildings and a museum

showing history of the site.

Market Hall
Near town centre
Now a centre for local crafts and
shops.

**Museum of Royal Welch
Fusiliers**
Military museum inside castle,
with many mementoes of the
regiment's past.

At the southern end of the Menai Straits is the historic town of **Caernarfon**. It is probably the best known of all the towns in North Wales, and stands in a magnificent position at the foot of the mountains overlooking Anglesey. The castle, built by Edward I, is one of the greatest (and most attractive) castles in the country. It stands above the busy quayside as a reminder of the strategic importance of this bustling town. Traditionally the castle is where Edward II was invested as the first Prince of Wales after his birth there in 1284. The castle has in more recent times seen the investitures as Prince of Wales of the future Edward VIII (in 1911) and of Prince Charles (in 1969).

Unusually, the castle has thirteen polygonal towers and banded masonry and although outwardly perfect it is internally just a shell. Like all castles in this region it has had a stormy career, playing a significant part in the wars between the Welsh and English princes. It was twice unsuccessfully beseiged by Owain Glyndwr; in the Civil War it stood for the king, and when captured by Cromwell's troops it was ordered to be destroyed in 1660. This warrant was fortunately never exercised and it stands now as a magnificent reminder of the castle builder's craft. In the Queen's Tower within the walls is the Museum of the Royal Welch Fusiliers, with many mementoes from

A doorway in Caernarfon with a naive carving of an angel carrying a coat of arms

the history of the regiment.

As at Conwy, much of the town wall survives, built with the castle as part of an integrated defensive system. It surrounds the old parts of the town, the narrow streets forming a regular pattern within. In the north-west corner, and built into the walls, is the chantry of St Mary which utilised the adjoining tower as a vestry and bell tower. There are many fine old buildings enclosed by the walls, including the Black Boy Inn, a traditional public house with some good local dishes, and the old Market Hall which now is more a centre for local crafts than a market.

Until very recently the town, like many along the coast, was blighted by traffic, but the building of a new bypass has considerably relieved the congestion, thus allowing visitors to wander at a more leisurely pace than previously. Castle Square, which is now relatively free from traffic, has a Saturday market and is an ideal base

Caernarfon Castle

to explore the town.

The Romans also appreciated the value of the site's strategic importance, or perhaps they just found it slightly less hostile than the mountains inland. They built a fort just to the south of the present town, half a mile out, on the road to Beddgelert. Little now remains but the foundations give a good idea of the ground plan. On the site is an excellent museum covering the history of the fort and the organization of the Roman army in Britain and other related subjects. The fort, known as *Segontium*, was occupied from about AD78 to AD380 when the Roman troops withdrew from Britain. During that time a sizeable community had grown up outside the walls and on retirement many of the soldiers are believed to have settled and farmed in the area. It was a fort well integrated with local life.

The view south from Caernarfon and Bangor is of the mountains. They are not large by comparison with other European mountain ranges but they always give an overriding impression of grandeur. They form the northern end of the Snowdonia National Park and are divided into three distinct ranges, separated by deep valleys. To the east, bounded on one side by the Conwy Valley and on the other by the Nant Ffrancon Pass, are the Carneddau; in the centre are the Glyders; and on the west, the highest of all, is Snowdon with its surrounding mountains. In all there are fourteen peaks over 3,000ft, all linked by footpaths.

The mountains, originally formed more than 300 million years ago, are the worn down stumps of much higher mountains. They have been folded by earth movements to more than 20,000ft and then gradually worn by changing temperatures, water and ice to their present size. The valleys have been carved by ancient glaciers and many of the hanging valleys, called cwms, have been dammed by glacial deposits to hold lakes. The debris of glaciers is scattered around the hillsides and in moraines along and across the valleys. The alpine plants left by the receding ice in some of the high cwms provide a living link with the Ice Age and show how little these mountains have changed despite man's interference.

Snowdon is the highest mountain in England and Wales. With its sharp ridges and sombre cwms, it is inevitable that stories have grown around it. This is the land of the legendary King Arthur. Yr Wyddfa, the highest peak, is traditionally the tomb of Rhita Fawr

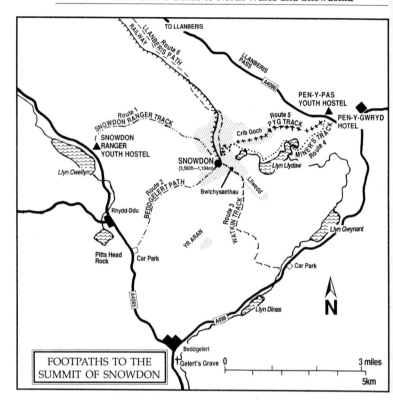

FOOTPATHS TO THE SUMMIT OF SNOWDON

slain by Arthur. Arthur is supposed to have fought his last battle at the Pass of Arrows (Bwlch y Saethau) below Snowdon's summit; Llyn Llydaw by tradition is the lake into which Excalibur was thrown. On the slopes above is a cave in which three of King Arthur's knights rest, ready to come to the aid of the country when needed. Despite the legends, what is more certain is that several of the Welsh princes retreated into the area when defeated, for it proved a most hostile environment to the pursuing English troops.

The Snowdon Massif, known more traditionally by the Welsh as Yr Eryri, is a star-shaped cluster of peaks connected by a series of steep ridges, the highest, Yr Wyddfa at 3,560ft, is in the centre and

FOOTPATHS TO THE SUMMIT OF SNOWDON

ROUTE 1
Snowdon Ranger Track: $3^3/_4$ miles. An easy path with delightful views, zig-zags above youth hostel.

ROUTE 2
Beddgelert Path: $3^3/_4$ miles. Easy to follow, climbs gradually to summit, Steeper near top.

ROUTE 3
Watkin Track: $3^1/_2$ miles. Most interesting, but hardest walk. Good path at first up to Bwlch y Saethau, steep and loose after that. A long climb.

ROUTE 4
Miner's Track: $3^3/_4$ miles. Follows copper miners' track to lake, then rises more steeply to join PYG track to summit. Good for introduction to the mountain if you do not wish to go to the top.

ROUTE 5
PYG (Pen-y-Gwryd) Track: $3^1/_4$ miles. Good route. Climbs quickly and then contours around cwm. Zig-zags below summit. A well-made path. Recommended favourite route.

ROUTE 6
Llanberis Path: 5 miles. Follows close to railway. Starts in Llanberis and climbs gradually. Not the most interesting route. Easy but long.

generally the object of most people's attention. The main routes to the summit are fairly easy underfoot though can be arduous to those unused to hill walking. Many thousands reach the summit each year, though to enjoy the walk a certain amount of fitness is recommended.

North of Yr Wyddfa is the summit of Crib-y-Ddysgl (3,493ft) leading out on the narrow ridge to Crib Goch (3,023ft) in the north-

Snowdon and Llyn Llydaw

east. This is a splendid ridge to walk with towering pinnacles and buttresses and with superb situations, but is not for the inexperienced or faint hearted.

To the south-east is the craggy ridge of Lliwedd (2,497ft) with its steep walls overlooking Llyn Llydaw, and looking south is the long southern ridge leading out to Yr Aran (2,451ft) above the Gwynant Valley. There are good tracks across the ridges but care must be taken—the weather can be extremely inclement with gusting winds.

Many visitors are content to reach the summit by the rack-and-pinion railway which ascends the five miles from Llanberis with fantastic views en route. The railway was opened in 1896 and has a maximum gradient of 20 per cent, it was designed by Swiss engineers and uses Swiss locomotives.

For those who achieve the summit by whatever means the views, providing the weather is clear, are worth the effort. You are above every other mountain in England and Wales and can see many of them; the Welsh mountains and lakes are immediately obvious even down to Cadair Idris thirty miles to the south. Further afield to the west the Wicklow Hills of Ireland can be seen across the sea and to the north the Isle of Man and the Lake District, with the coast of Lancashire and Blackpool Tower visible. For more distant views a clear day and a good imagination is needed. There is a café and bar on the summit to reward thirsty walkers but be warned that it is only open when the train is running.

The ascent of the summit, Yr Wyddfa, has understandably been a popular achievement at least from early last century when George Borrow in his book *Wild Wales* describes how he walked up with his family in 1850 and even at that time 'there was a rude cabin in which refreshments are sold and in which a person resides throughout the year'.

There are six main routes up Snowdon, starting from car parks all around the mountain. Although some are easier and some are longer, all require much physical effort and a sound knowledge of mountain walking, for the weather can change drastically during the 5-8 hours of the walk. All the paths are well made and quite easy to follow if care is taken.

Perhaps the greatest expedition is the Snowdon Horseshoe, a traverse of all the main peaks to and from Pen-y-Pass. It involves

THINGS TO SEE AND DO AROUND LLANBERIS

Snowdon Mountain Railway
Runs a regular passenger service to the summit of Snowdon using steam powered rack-and-pinion locomotives.

Dolbadarn Castle
Home of the Welsh Princes in the twelfth century, it stands above the lake guarding the entrance to the Llanberis Pass.

Welsh Slate Museum
In the former workshops of Dinorwig Quarry, showing much of the original machinery and equipment used. Films and slides of quarry work.

Llanberis Lake Railway
Steam railway starting from the Slate Museum, running along lakeside through country park.

Padarn Country Park
On shore of the lake with native oak trees and walks through quarry remains.

Dinorwig Power Station
Information centre, hugh cavern inside mountain with guided tours (but no children under 14).

Museum of the North
Devoted to natural environment of Snowdonia and Welsh history.

steep climbing and knife-edge ridges following the rim of the cwm surrounding Llyn Llydaw and taking in the summits of Crib-Goch (3,023ft), Crib-y-Ddysgl (3,493ft) over Yr Wyddfa (3,560ft) before descending to Bwlch-y-Saethau and the steep crags of Lliwedd (2,947ft) and thence back down the Miners' Track to Pen-y-Pass. It must be stressed that this is a major undertaking and should not be attempted without a stout pair of boots, a head for heights and much previous experience; the weather and rock conditions should be checked before attempting this marvellous expedition.

H
6-7h
****
††††

Pen-y-Pass, the highest point of the Llanberis Pass, and the starting point for many of the Snowdon walks, is the site of the old Gorphwysfa Hotel, an old coaching inn converted some years ago to a youth hostel. In the early part of the century the hotel was the centre for the pioneer rock climbers who visited the many crags on the slopes of Snowdon. The road descends steeply from there down to the south-east to the Pen y Gwryd Hotel, which superseded

Lliwedd from Snowdon

 it as the meeting place for climbers. Both the youth hostel and the hotel are Mountain Rescue points. To the north of Pen-y-Pass the road winds down the Llanberis Pass, between the huge rock buttresses which are the playgrounds of the modern rock climbers, to Llyn Peris and Llyn Padarn.

Llyn Peris has recently been drained and dammed to form the bottom lake of the huge Dinorwig Pump Storage Power Station. This hydro-electric scheme involves the use of two lakes, one high lake and one lower reservoir. The top lake, Marchlyn Mawr, behind Elidir Fawr to the north, stores the water until generating capacity is needed. The water is then released and drives the turbines built under the hillside opposite and flows into the lower lake, Llyn Peris. During off peak times, using surplus electricity from the National Grid, the water is then pumped back to the higher lake for future use. It is a massive project involving deep underground workings and tunnels, well hidden in the slate quarries and underground, but the entrance to the power station is visible across Llyn Peris. The electricity is fed into the national grid. There is an excellent informa-

Snowdon and Llyn Padarn from Brynrefail

tion centre at the power station and visitors can see the massive underground workings. It is a huge project and is well recommended visiting.

Llanberis, in the bottom of the valley, sits almost between the two lakes and is probably best known as the starting point for the Snowdon Mountain Railway. This is a rack-and-pinion railway carrying passengers to the summit of Snowdon; as an easy alternative to walking, it is very popular. Not far from the station is the Welsh Slate Museum, with exhibits and buildings relating to all aspects of quarry work. The old quarry railway has been rebuilt to provide a pleasant run along the north shore of Llyn Padarn through a country park of the same name. It is a narrow gauge railway and many of the original locomotives are still in use.

On a small hill above the town sits the round keep of Dolbadarn Castle built in the early thirteenth century, it is thought for Llewelyn The Great, while on the opposite side of the lake can be seen the huge tiers of the old Dinorwig Slate Mine which rise for 1,500ft up the side of the mountain. The mine now houses the aforementioned Pump Storage Power Station.

To the north of the town and above the massive slate tips rise the bulky slopes of Elidir Fawr and the Glyder range of mountains, most of which are over 3,000ft high. They are accessible on foot from the Llanberis side, but the most interesting walks and ascents are made from the north, starting mainly from Llyn Ogwen, where there are several convenient car parks. There is no village at **Ogwen** just a collection of buildings comprising a youth hostel and an adventure school — but it is easy to get the feel of the high mountains despite the busy main road. The old packhorse road runs parallel to the modern road and can be traced for much of the distance along the valley side. It makes a fine walk in magnificent surroundings and is fairly level and easy to follow. The remains of the old packhorse bridge can be seen underneath the more modern road bridge by the falls below Llyn Ogwen.

Access to the Glyders is by a footpath which climbs steeply from behind Ogwen Cottage, a Mountain Rescue Post, before levelling out into Cwm Idwal. The path then follows the shores of Llyn Idwal past the Idwal Slabs, perhaps some of the most frequently climbed rocks in Britain. It climbs steeply to Twll Du or Devil's Kitchen, a

Tryfan and Glyder Fach

narrow defile of black rock which seems to cut the mountain in half. The whole of Cwm Idwal is a nature reserve with many rare species of alpine plants and orchids found amongst the rocks. It was the early botanists who started the sport of rock climbing as they searched higher and higher for new specimens.

A pleasant afternoon can be enjoyed without leaving the cwm but the higher mountains, are steep and rocky, though in many respects totally different from their neighbours.

Climbing on past Devil's Kitchen the path comes to a small lake (Llyn-y-Cwn) and then divides. To the right the track climbs easily to the summit of Y Garn (3,104ft) then along the crest to Mynydd Perfedd and either west above Marchlyn Mawr, the top lake of the pump storage scheme, to Elidir Fawr (3,029ft) or north to Carnedd-y-Filiast and down into Bethesda.

H
2-3h
****
†††

Taking the track on the left from Llyn-y-Cwn and going south-east, the path rises steeply up the scree-covered slopes of Glyder Fawr (3,279ft) to the summit, a rather desolate boulder-strewn plateau. It continues along the ridge past the well-named Castell-y-Gwynt (Castle of the Winds) to Glyder Fach (3,262ft) and the flat

H
5+h
****
††††

The Llanberis Pass

Narrow gauge steam locomotives from the Llanberis Lake Railway at the Welsh Slate Museum

Cwm Idwal and the Idwal Slabs

stone of the Cantilever, a perched block which seems delicately balanced but has so far defied all the efforts of large and small parties to dislodge it.

The views from both these summits are some of the finest in Snowdonia, looking down on the surrounding mountains and valleys, with the summit of Tryfan seemingly only a step away to the east. The path descends steeply alongside the Bristly Ridge to the cwm and then north back to Ogwen. However the summit of Tryfan

(3,010ft), only a short scramble above, is well worth the extra effort, for this is one of the true mountains of North Wales. With a sharp profile from every viewpoint it stands separated from all others above the valley. On this ascent one's hands will be needed for extra grip, as the path to the top is steep and rocky. The summit is crowned by two great monoliths, imaginatively known as Adam and Eve. They are close together and it is said that a true Welsh mountaineer is one who has stepped from one to the other. With the steep drop below it is safer not to attempt it, but to descend by the much slower, but safer, route back to the cwm, and then north down to Ogwen Cottage.

Between the Nant Ffrancon Pass and Llyn Ogwen and the Conwy Valley is the largest range of hills, which rise steeply above the lake mainly north from Pen-yr-Oleu-wen (3,211ft) to Drum (2,529ft), then sloping more gently on the east to the foothills above Conwy. They are of a completely different character, being more rounded and grass-covered, with only occasional steep cliffs and cwms. The walking is more arduous and the route finding more difficult. As it is a large area with many access points, it is suggested that those considering mountain walking here should equip themselves with a large scale map to gain maximum enjoyment.

H
3h
****
†††

Despite this advice, it would be unfair not to give at least a brief description of these hills. The main path ascends from the west end of Llyn Ogwen and rises very steeply for almost 2,000ft to the summit of Pen-yr-Oleu-wen (3,211ft). Once this has been achieved, there is little further climbing for the whole length of the ridge. Circling round the very edge of one of the most perfect cwms, Ffynnon Lloer, the summit of Carnedd Dafydd (3,427ft) is soon reached; then on to Carnedd Llewelyn (3,458ft). From there a spur goes east providing some interesting and mainly downhill walking, and for those who have had enough there is a circular return route to the valley. Going north from Carnedd Llewelyn, the ridge can be followed over Foel Grach (3,196ft), Foel Fras and then down to Drum (2,529ft). This is a full day's excursion, and it is best to arrange transport at the northern end, if a long walk back is to be avoided.

The smaller hills to the south of the main range are split by a series of deep valleys, each containing a lake of individual character dammed to provide water for industry in the Conwy Valley. The

PLACES OF INTEREST IN AND AROUND BETWS-Y-COED

Waterloo Bridge
Built in the same year as the Battle of Waterloo, a superb cast iron bridge carrying the A5 over the river.

Swallow Falls
Good views of tumbling cataract just by the A5 above the village.

National Park Visitor Centre
Large and colourful exhibition on Snowdonia. Children's room, information desk, slide presentations and craft displays.

Conwy Valley Railway Museum
Housed in a purpose-built building adjacent to the station, with many items showing all aspects of railway life.

Capel Garmon
Burial chamber with remains of long barrow. North of A5, follow signs to Capel Garmon.

northernmost, Llyn Eigian, burst its dam in 1925 causing a disastrous flood; the great masonry blocks and deep fissure created can be seen just below the remaining lake. The next, Llyn Cowlyd, is set in bleak uplands, while the two smaller ones to the south, Llyn Crafnant and Llyn Geirionnydd, are in wooded valleys. The latter is a popular spot for daytrippers, yachtsmen and water skiers, though the roar of power boats upsets the serenity of this beautiful spot. All these valleys, with the exception of Cowlyd, can be reached easily by road from the Conwy Valley.

To the south is the **Gwydyr Forest** stretching from Llyn Crafnant to Penmachno and covering many of the hills and valley sides. The forests have been developed since 1921 by the Forestry Commission and are now a Forest Park with free access. They are a fine introduction to the wilder mountains beyond.

There are many footpaths through the forest, some following long forgotten roads to old lead mines and quarries, while others follow delightful little streams to quiet mountain lakes — everybody is welcome provided that they respect the forest and natural environment. As the forest has many old copper and lead mines, care must be taken when walking near the shafts.

The Afon Llugwy at Betws-y-Coed

Capel Garmon burial chamber, high above Betws-y-Coed

The small town of **Betws-y-Coed** is almost surrounded by the forest at the junction of three valleys, the Lledr Valley from the south, the Llugwy Valley from the east and the Conwy Valley to the north. It sits astride the A5 trunk road and is a frequent bottleneck in summer as most of the traffic has to cross the graceful Waterloo Bridge. This cast iron bridge was built in 1815 and carries the inscription in large letters: 'This Arch was Constructed in the Same Year the Battle of Waterloo was Fought', as well as decorative flowers in the spandrels. There are hotels, cafes and many craft shops, while near the railway station is the Conwy Valley Railway Museum. The Tourist Information Centre has descriptive leaflets of the many short walks in the locality and in the nearby forest.

The main road rises through the town and just on the left is an old stone bridge with a small cataract below it — if you are lucky you may see salmon jumping. A few miles upstream and next to the road, are the Swallow Falls, a magnificent sight particularly after rainfall. The next village, **Capel Curig**, is merely a cross roads with a few climbing and other shops and several hotels. The imposing

The Waterloo Bridge, Betws-y-Coed

H
3-4h
**
†††

mountain across the lake is Moel Siabod; from this side it is one of the easier mountain walks. Start about one mile towards Betws-y-Coed at Pont Cyfyng where a small road turns off to a cluster of cottages. The main track begins there and follows an old quarry road which at first rises easily past the slate quarries and then follows the ridge with some easy scrambling to the grass slopes below the rocky summit cairn. There are fine views over the sheer drop to the cwm below. The path along and down the ridge to the Pen-y-Gwryd Hotel gives a long walk; it is best to return the way you came for the views are always different on the way back.

Just outside Capel Curig is Plas-y-Brenin, the National Mountaineering Centre, which provides courses in all grades of walking, climbing and skiing in the surrounding mountains, and canoeing on the nearby lake and river. The centre is open to the public with indoor climbing walls and at the back a dry ski slope. Many courses are introductory and even the most inexperienced can participate.

Past Plas-y-Brenin the road skirts the shores of Llynau Mymbyr and continues up the long glaciated valley with one of the finest

Plas-y-Brenin, the National Mountaineering Centre, with its dry ski slope

views of Snowdon directly ahead. Looking into the horseshoe formed by the Crib Coch ridge to the right and Lliwedd to the left you look directly up to the majestic summit in the centre, from here it always looks forbidding and sombre.

Coming to the junction at the Pen-y-Gwryd Hotel continue ahead to Nant Gwynant, the road to the right going over Pen-y-Pass and thence to the Llanberis Pass. As already mentioned the hotel at the junction was the training headquarters for the first successful team to conquer Mount Everest in 1953. The main room in the bar has the signatures of these climbers on the ceiling. It is a comfortable hotel and has long been the centre for the local Mountain Rescue Team. Across the road on a small hillock is the square base of a Roman fort which controlled the ancient routeways over this pass, though a less hospitable posting could hardly be found for men brought up on the Mediterranean coast.

The road ahead descends easily to **Nant Gwynant** passing a viewpoint on the right. It is worth a stop for perhaps the finest view of Snowdon and the valley. Below is Llyn Gwynant above the

The peak of Moel Siabod from the head of the Afon Glaslyn

*Entrance to the
Sygun Copper Mine*

brooding shape of Yr Wyddfa. Continuing on you pass Llyn Gwynant, with its canoeists and windsurfers and Llyn Dinas, always quiet and peaceful and after a few miles arrive at the lovely village of Beddgelert.

Between Llyn Gwynant and Beddgelert is the Sygun Copper Mine which has recently been reopened as a visitor attraction. Visitors are taken along levels and up ladderways, rediscovering the old passageways which had been abandoned so long ago. On the surface it is possible to see the remains of some of the old buildings, reclaimed from a dense rhododendron undergrowth. There is a small café here and video-corner where details of the mine and its reopening may be seen.

Standing at the confluence of two rivers which join to become

PLACES OF INTEREST IN AND AROUND BEDDGELERT

Gelert's Grave
A short walk along the riverbank to legendary grave that gave the village its name.

Sygun Copper Mine
Guided tours around nineteenth-century copper mine and caves with views of Gwynant Valley. Visitor Centre on site. Short or long walks in beautiful surroundings, particularly along river on disused line of old Snowdon Light Railway.

The 'grave' of Gelert, Prince Llewelyn's faithful dog

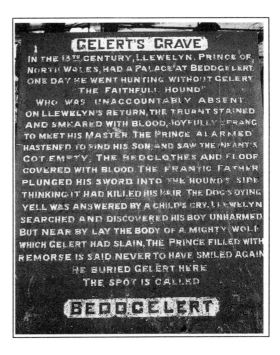

GELERT'S GRAVE

IN THE 13TH CENTURY, LLEWELYN, PRINCE OF NORTH WALES, HAD A PALACE AT BEDDGELERT. ONE DAY HE WENT HUNTING WITHOUT GELERT "THE FAITHFUL HOUND" WHO WAS UNACCOUNTABLY ABSENT ON LLEWELYN'S RETURN, THE TRUANT STAINED AND SMEARED WITH BLOOD, JOYFULLY SPRANG TO MEET HIS MASTER. THE PRINCE ALARMED HASTENED TO FIND HIS SON, AND SAW THE INFANT'S COT EMPTY, THE BEDCLOTHES AND FLOOR COVERED WITH BLOOD. THE FRANTIC FATHER PLUNGED HIS SWORD INTO THE HOUND'S SIDE THINKING IT HAD KILLED HIS HEIR. THE DOG'S DYING YELL WAS ANSWERED BY A CHILD'S CRY. LLEWELYN SEARCHED AND DISCOVERED HIS BOY UNHARMED BUT NEAR BY LAY THE BODY OF A MIGHTY WOLF WHICH GELERT HAD SLAIN. THE PRINCE FILLED WITH REMORSE IS SAID NEVER TO HAVE SMILED AGAIN HE BURIED GELERT HERE THE SPOT IS CALLED

BEDDGELERT

the Afon Glaslyn, **Beddgelert** is a bustling village torn between the tourist trade and the chaos the traffic it brings can cause. It is nevertheless relatively unspoilt and at the heart of the mountains.

The village thrives on the story of the legendary Gelert, a dog belonging to Prince Llewelyn which he slew after returning from a hunting trip on finding that his son was missing and the dog was covered in blood. It was only later that his son was found safe and a wolf dead nearby, obviously killed by the dog. He buried the faithful hound and the 'grave' is just a short stroll alongside the river from the village centre. A similar story appears in other parts of the world, and it is most likely that it was introduced here by an over-zealous publican in the eighteenth century to encourage visitors. It is more probable that the Gelert referred to in the village name was an early Christian connected with a priory which once stood on that site.

L
1-1½h
*
†††

Beddgelert is an ideal centre for exploring the surrounding hills, for there are some fine hotels and guest houses; though a little crowded in summer, it has a charm of its own. The old Welsh Highland Railway passed close to the village. A pleasant stroll links up with this by following the signs from the village to Gelert's grave and continuing alongside the river banks to cross the old railway bridge and then along the railway (now disused) to Aberglaslyn. Then a series of tunnels brings one to Nantmor. For a long (about 9 miles), easy, but excellent walk one continues through Nantmor on the minor road, which traces the course of an old road to the junction. Turn left and follow that road past Cae Dafydd Craft Centre and Farm (with tea shop) along the valley with its bubbling stream to pass the slate quarries and descend to Nant Gwynant. A footpath can be followed along the banks of the river and around Llyn Dinas back to Beddgelert.

L
4h
*
††

M
2+h
**
††††

A variation on this route can be made after emerging from the long tunnel on the railway. Turn left here and follow a good footpath up Cwm Bychan to some old copper mines and the remains of a bucket conveyor. The path then goes off to the left, across a small hollow, to the ridge above Nant Gwynant and then descends the old miners' track to a minor road and thence back to Beddgelert. There are many short and simple walks around the village. It is usually best to enquire locally about walks for the route very much depends on the time available.

South of Beddgelert, and downstream, is the well known **Aberglaslyn Pass** which must feature more often on calendars

Beddgelert

Cnicht and the Moelwyns

The castle folly at Llanfrothen

than any other place in Wales. It has all the components of a classic beauty spot. A steep sided valley, trees, a tumbling river and a bridge all combine perfectly and can be viewed with little effort from the roadside. At one time ships could sail right up to the bridge, but since the building of the embankment across the mouth of the estuary, the land has been reclaimed and the river is impassable from Porthmadog.

The hills to the east of Aberglaslyn are fairly easily accessible on minor roads which branch off the main road from there to Penrhyndeudraeth. The first road up the Nantmor valley has several picnic spots and small parking areas; it is a beautiful area, but the road is narrow. From the high point on that road, where there is an old slate quarry, a good little path opposite a white cottage goes up to Llyn Llagi. The path continues beyond the lake and over the shoulder to Llyn-yr-Adar and on to the ridge of Cnicht. This can be traversed with wonderful views of the estuary and descended until the path breaks off to the right at a col below a small crag. It joins an old packhorse trail which, if followed to the right, goes downhill

H
3+h
**
††††

to the road following a lovely little stream back to the quarry. Several other footpaths leave this road for other lakes, and they are all fairly easy walking but as they may be damp underfoot, it is best to go well shod.

Cnicht, sometimes called the Matterhorn of North Wales, is best seen from the south, and with Moelwyn Bach and Moelwyn Mawr it stands proudly above the estuary. **Croesor**, a small village at the end of a minor road, is the starting point for any walks on that range. The road to Croesor starts by a large gatehouse in Llanfrothen. It is narrow and high walled and passes Plas Brodanw, home of the late Sir Clough Williams-Ellis the architect, best known for the hotel and village of Portmeirion. Opposite the house a gate leads uphill to a small castle with superb views over the estuary; it is a 'folly', being the architect's wedding present from his brother officers during his time in the army. It is a short but very pleasant stroll.

From the car park at Croesor there is a well signposted track which follows the ridge to the top of Cnicht. It is an easy walk, with one difficult scrambling section just below the summit, but if care is taken it should present no problems. The walk is recommended for its ease and views.

H
3h
**
†††

Moelwyn Mawr is best tackled by following the old quarry road beyond the village to the highest quarry, which until recently had a fine collection of buildings still surviving. From the back of the quarry the footpath up and over the shoulder brings one to the top, before descending down the ridge to the south and directly to the village.

H
3-4h
**
†††

Moelwyn Bach, the smaller of the two, can be approached from the south through a small forestry plantation at the high point of the road linking Croesor and Rhyd. The path is not too clear and it is wet underfoot, but once the ridge is reached walking is drier and straightforward: the views from the summit are magnificent; for ease it is suggested that the descent is made by the same route.

H
3h
**
†††

There are many fine walks in this area and it is ideal for a good day out. There are also numerous abandoned quarries and slate mines to interest the industrial archaeologist. These hills are less frequented than those to the north, but there is still much to see and enjoy, though proper dress and equipment are essential.

5

THE LLEYN PENINSULA

In stunning contrast to the mountains of Snowdonia is the Lleyn peninsula to the west, stretching like a long finger towards Ireland. Some twenty-five miles long and between five and ten miles wide it is an area of outstanding beauty and given the more temperate weather it is accustomed to, can compare with any coastline throughout Europe.

It is a land of rolling scenery, dark hills and beautiful coves and beaches. Despite the influx of visitors in summer it has retained its Welsh charm and language. Close to the hills and well provided with facilities for the visitor it can be an ideal base for touring or for those who enjoy a relaxed holiday but occasionally like a good day on the hills. With easy access to the beaches and bays it will suit the boating enthusiast. There are cliffs for the climber, bird watcher and botanist and golf courses for those who enjoy more athletic pursuits.

Divided from the bulk of Snowdonia by a range of hills of grand stature but limited height it has much to occupy the visitor. For those who like to explore the landscape this area is steeped in history both prehistoric and from the more recent Celtic period. Walkers can enjoy the sharp hills or a coastal jaunt. All around there is a great feeling of openness, the sky seems to dominate all the scenery.

For convenience, the Caernarfon-Porthmadog road will be re-

The Nantlle ridge

garded as the eastern boundary of the area. It is a pleasant road ascending gradually from suburban Caernarfon past the old Roman fort of *Segontium* and following the course of the ancient Roman road into the heart of Snowdonia. Heading south the sharp bulk of Mynydd Mawr on the right has the profile of an elephant. Passing below the trunk and along the shores of Llyn Cwellyn and the Snowdon Ranger Youth Hostel, once famous for its 'Ranger' who led walkers to the nearby summit of Snowdon, the road arrives at Rhyd-Ddu.

Turning right, to the west, leads up to **Bwlchgylfin** which gives relatively easy access for walkers to this superb range of hills. Close to the summit of the pass is Llyn-y-Dywarchen, a diminutive lake which was once one of the wonders of Wales. It had a legendary floating island which could carry cattle across the lake; visitors came from far and wide to see this spectacle which is sadly no longer evident.

From the top of the pass, a rather gloomy place, the view to the west is one of slate waste and huge tips. What devastation man has

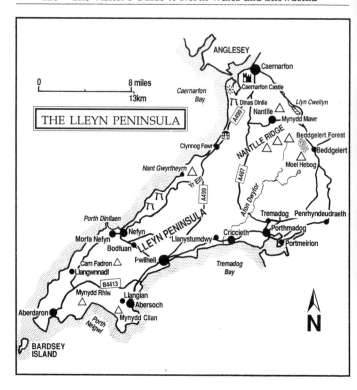

THE LLEYN PENINSULA

created in the pursuit of money! Around the village of **Nantlle** many of these huge craters have now filled with water, but efforts are being made to restore the machinery and workings of one mine above the village.

H
3h
**
††

For the summit of Mynydd Mawr go north on the path which leaves from the top of the pass and follow it from the western end of the lake near a small building. It rises easily at first through a miniature rocky pass up an easy grass slope until it narrows towards the summit with views straight down to Llyn Cwellyn. The descent is by the same route.

To the south of the pass rises Y Garn, a spur of Mynydd Drws-y-Coed, the northernmost peak of the Nantlle ridge. The traverse of the ridge is an excellent day's walking, covering in all five peaks over 2,000ft. The route is not difficult to follow with the aid of a good map and compass, but for many it will be a major expedition and is outside the scope of this guide.

H
aa
day
***
††††

South from Rhyd-Ddu stretches the **Beddgelert Forest**, covering much of the lower slopes of Moel Hebog. The Forestry Commission has done much to encourage people to use the forest; there is an excellent camp site and caravan site, a visitor information centre and shop. Available at the shop is an orienteering map of the forest — for those who have never tried the sport it is an excellent introduction and a good way to spend the afternoon, testing their navigational skills and exploring the forest, but old clothes are essential.

L
$1/_2$-3h
*
†††

From the car park in the forest starts one of several paths leading up **Moel Hebog** (2,566ft). It is one of the friendliest mountains in the area, with certainly some of the finest views. The path is clear for most of the way, following the stream right up through the forest, until breaking clear just below a small crag on the left. Half way up the crag, and reached by a tricky scramble is Ogof (cave of) Owain Glyndwr. Overlooking the valley this cave is reputed to be the hide-out of the Welsh fourteenth-century leader but it is so small and damp that it hardly befits the hero's grandeur. On the same crag, but much easier to reach, is a small hollow in the cliff, which is a disused asbestos mine, though the narrow seam must have proved uneconomic.

H
3-5h
**
††††

The path continues more steeply now to the col, and at a wall one turns left for Moel Hebog and right for Moel Lefn (2,094ft), a minor summit that is worth climbing. The summit of Moel Hebog is reached after a steep climb alongside the wall. The views are magnificent: to the north lies the Nantlle ridge; to the east the Snowdon Range and in the distance Moel Siabod, Cnicht and the Moelwyns: south are the Rhinogs and Tremadog Bay; while to the west the Lleyn Peninsula is at one's feet and on a clear day the coast of Ireland can be seen.

One can descend by the same route but it is better to return eastwards down the path to Cwm Cloch farm and Beddgelert and then walk about a mile back to the forest. The route is equally enjoyable if started from Beddgelert, where the path starts just out on the road

Tremadog

Porthmadog Harbour

The Festiniog Railway at Porthmadog Station

to Rhyd-Ddu. Cross the river and go up the lane to a farm at Cwm Cloch. A signpost on the end of the barn directs one up the path which rises easily at first but becomes more steep near the summit.

South of Moel Hebog the lower hills give some pleasant rambling: but as paths are scarce one has to pick one's route carefully.

All give excellent views particularly over the reclaimed estuary of Traeth Mawr to the south. The estuary of the Afon Glaslyn, known as Traeth Mawr, was once said to be the most beautiful in the whole of Wales. It is now about 7,000 acres of reclaimed land, and is frequently flooded after heavy rain. It was created by the building of an embankment (the Cob) across its mouth in 1811 by William Madocks MP. At one time the estuary was navigable up the Aberglaslyn Bridge. Madocks' intention was to create an easy crossing point for traffic to the Lleyn Peninsula in order to open it up for the Irish trade. He also hoped to dry out the enclosed land for farming. His first intention never succeeded, the second has to a certain extent, providing grazing land only.

Madocks built the village of **Tremadog**, and later Porthmadog to be the port for his great plans. Both names have now been converted to the Welsh, so apart from a statue in Porthmadog little evidence remains of his influence on the project. He lived at Tan-yr-Allt above Tremadog and the village was laid out to please him. The poet Shelley was a frequent guest at the house and T. E. Lawrence (Lawrence of Arabia) was born in the village. The village is still of interest to architects and builders, its stone houses neatly built on each side of a square. Below the cliffs what looks like a town hall was in fact a theatre with access from the adjoining hotel on one side, with the cottage at the other end as the changing rooms; it is now a craft shop.

Behind the village, though hidden from the road by woodlands, and stretching for about one mile are Tremadog Rocks. They are a favourite area for rock climbing, particularly if it is raining further inland. The woods at the bottom are a nature reserve, much of it being natural growth with native trees.

Porthmadog was originally planned to be the lesser of the two towns but grew to pre-eminence with the opening of the port. A railway was built across the Cob to the mines at Ffestiniog, so that slates could be exported from the quay. It was intended to be a great cultural centre as well as a port, which no doubt explains why the scheme received the enthusiastic backing of Shelley. The slate trade died when the mines were closed, so that even the old slate sheds have gone — now replaced by holiday flatlets on the quayside. The railway is still running as the famous Festiniog

PLACES TO VISIT IN AND AROUND PORTHMADOG

Maritime Museum
Porthmadog
Based on the sailing ketch
Garlandstone, has displays of
ships and seamen of Gwynedd.
Slate sheds as they used to be.

Porthmadog Pottery
At the end of Snowdon Street,
off the High Street.
Demonstrations of all stages of
pottery making, visitors can
have a go themselves.

Festiniog Railway
Porthmadog
Start of steam railway to
Blaenau Ffestiniog and also
small railway museum and gift
shop on the quay

Tyn Llan Pottery
Penmorfa
Displays of crafts and pottery
from all over Wales. Snacks and
tea available, with picnic spot.
Off A487 north of Tremadog

Brynkir Woollen Mills
Dolbenmaen. East of A487, 5
miles north of Tremadog.
Weavers of tapestries, bed-
spreads and smaller items in
traditional patterns.

Welsh Highland Railway
Tremadog Road, Porthmadog.
Steam trains and workshops,
limited service but great plans
for the future.

Railway, with its terminus on the quayside. The railway, which used
the anglicised version of Ffestiniog without the double 'f', was built
in 1836 and has the distinction of being the oldest narrow gauge
railway in the world. Originally the trucks loaded with slate descended from the quarries under gravity, and the empty ones
hauled back up by horses. It was the first narrow gauge line to
introduce steam locomotives, in 1863, and the first to use the
'Fairlie' type of double locomotives which were articulated in the
middle to accommodate the very tight curves. These unusual steam
locomotives are still in use as well as a number of more conven-
tional ones. The $13^3/_4$-mile journey rises over 700ft and there are
fine views from the train.

The port has now been taken over by yachtsmen, but because
of the silting of the estuary they must choose their sailing times by

the tide. Until recent years it was a pleasant little harbour to stroll around, but there is now little of interest, though with the opening of a Maritime Museum in an original sailing ship, efforts are being made to revitalise it. The town has a busy shopping centre with many Welsh craft shops to entice the visitor, and a pottery on the outskirts of the town where all are welcome to try their hand.

Several beaches are easily reached from the town centre; the nearest just around the headland is Borth-y-Gest, which has fine golden sands and small coves, but bathing is not too safe as the estuary is tidal. Next to it is Morfa Bychan or Black Rock Sands, much safer for bathing but more dangerous for walking. This is a two-mile stretch of wide flat beach backed by a large caravan site; car parking is allowed on the beach.

L
¹/₂-2h
*
†††

Just inland is the grand little hill of Moel-y-Gest, which is a pleasant viewpoint from which to survey the coast. There are several signposted footpaths which take no more than half an hour to the summit.

H
2h
**
†††

Several minor roads leave the main Caernarfon road (A4085) about two miles outside Tremadog. The first goes up to Cwm Ystradllyn past the magnificent ruin of a slate mill and then up to a reservoir. Parking is possible at the end of the road, and the hill in front is an easier alternative route to the summit of Moel Hebog. The peaceful valley may be explored by following the unmetalled road. The retaining wall below the slate tip has a superb curve.

The road to the north passes Brynkir Woollen Mills (open to the public) where Welsh tapestries, flannels and tweeds are woven, and continues up to Cwm Pennant. This is a beautiful little valley as it winds right into the hills with lots of tumbling streams and places to walk or picnic. It is also possible to reach this valley by turning off the main road at Dolbenmaen just past the castle mound.

Criccieth, the next town along the coast, is a popular resort with several good beaches; the one immediately in front of the town is a good place to launch a dinghy or swim. Above the harbour is the only major castle on the Lleyn peninsula and though little remains apart from the gateway it looks impressive from any angle. It is not one of Edward I's castles, being merely enlarged by him on the site of an earlier Welsh fortress. From the castle the views are magnificent and with the well developed hotel trade in the town it is an

Ruined slate mill at Cwm Ystradllyn

The seashore at Criccieth

BEACHES ON THE LLEYN PENINSULA'S SOUTH COAST

Near Porthmadog
Borth-y-Gest: Small bays and coves and tidal estuary.
Black Rock Sands: Two miles of good wide sands, safe bathing, drive your car onto the beach. Very popular and backed by caravan sites.

Criccieth
Two fine beaches divided by castle, safe bathing and launching facilities for small boats.

Pwllheli
Two safe beaches:
Gimblet Rock to south, shingle and sand;
Glandol beach to east, safe and sandy.

Llanbedrog
Sandy bay sheltered by headland. Ideal for bathing, boating, fishing and walks on headland.

Abersoch
Popular seaside resort with miles of fine golden sands. Very popular but still quite charming. Yacht club and mooring facilities, a sailor's paradise.

Porth Neigwl (Hell's Mouth)
Open sandy beach about 4 miles long, plenty of room for everybody.

Aberdaron
Good beach with safe bathing and boating, last stop for the pilgrims on the way to Bardsey Island. Interesting old church on the edge of the beach. Good headland walks.

excellent centre for touring the peninsula and mountains. Lloyd George, the statesman and Prime Minister, knew Criccieth well, for he spent his childhood in **Llanystumdwy**, just two miles away. He was educated in the village and died at Ty Newydd, a house he owned above the Criccieth road. His grave, designed by Sir Clough Williams-Ellis, is beside the river close to the bridge. In the village is a small museum with many mementoes of him.

Shortly after Llanystumdwy, the road divides, that to the north providing a fast route across the Lleyn to Nefyn, while the main road continues to amble down the coast. About one mile after passing a holiday camp (day visitors are allowed), a small signpost directs one to Penarth Fawr, an interesting and attractive fifteenth-century

Grave of Lloyd George beside the river at Llanystumdwy

manor house. Consisting basically of one room, it is well preserved and generally fairly quiet.

Pwllheli, the administrative centre and largest town, is perhaps the capital of the Lleyn. It is an ancient Welsh borough which received its charter from the Black Prince in 1355, and although it now has little of historical interest, with its shops and beaches it is a popular centre for holidaymakers. The town and beach are separated by about half a mile and several centuries, the town being typically old Welsh and the houses along the promenade being a mixture of Victorian and modern. The harbour, protected by a hook of land which almost encloses it, is safe and, with Gimlet Rock at its entrance, easy to find.

The wide sandy bay at Abersoch

The sand and shingle beaches face south and stretch for almost five miles to Llanbedrog and its rocky point. The bathing is excellent along the whole coastline and once round the headland the beaches continue for several more miles along St Tudwal's Bay.

A few miles from Pwllheli along the road to Nefyn is **Bodfuan**, which was the abode of St Buan in the sixth century. The church has stained glass depicting St Cudfan receiving the body of the saint on Bardsey Island. Bodfuan Woods were once owned by Ann Boleyn and later Elizabeth I.

Back on the south coast, **Abersoch** is a favourite spot and the small town is now surrounded by caravan sites and holiday homes. It is a delightful little village with a small harbour, that has developed in the last twenty to thirty years as the centre for boating enthusiasts in North Wales. With two sheltered bays and wide safe beaches it is ideal for launching and sailing boats of all sizes.

Just off the coast are two small islands, no longer inhabited, known as St Tudwal's Islands, after the saint who founded a chapel there in the sixth century. Little remains of its Augustinian priory, and the islands are left to the birds and the lighthouse. Boat trips can be taken around the islands, thus also giving the opportunity to view the superb coastline from the sea.

Nearing the end of the Lleyn the villages seem to get smaller and more widely scattered. **Llangian**, near Abersoch, is of some interest as one of the best kept villages in the county and for the sixth-century stone in the churchyard carved in Latin commemorating Melus, the first mention of a doctor in Wales.

Three miles south-west of Abersoch is Mynydd Cilan, an open cliff-top area with wonderful views belonging to the National Trust. Then, crossing behind the long bay of Porth Neigwl or Hell's Mouth, the road climbs steeply over the shoulder of Mynydd Rhiw. The Plas yn Rhiw estate covers 400 acres and is criss-crossed by tracks and almost surrounded by roads. Rising to 999ft high, it has some pleasant walks with excellent views of the coastline. Early man may have appreciated the hill for the same reason, for there are several archaeological sites to be found on the hillside, including at the northern end a Stone Age axe factory. Towards Aberdaron the scenery is superb but somewhat marred by what seems like a forest of telegraph and electricity poles and their overhead lines.

Y Gegin Fawr, Aberdaron, where pilgrims ate before crossing to Bardsey Island

Aberdaron is a tiny village on the very edge of the sea, the last stop for the pilgrims on their way to Bardsey Island. A café and a souvenir shop, Y Gegin Fawr, the Big Kitchen, was formerly a hostel and resting place before the crossing, while the small church of St Hywyn, on the very edge of the shore, served their spiritual needs on the last lap. The double-naved church dates from the twelfth to fifteenth centuries. It was built on the site of an ancient Celtic oratory which was founded around the end of the fifth century by Hywyn, who is said to have come from Brittany with Cadfan, the founder of the monastery on Bardsey Island.

Bardsey Island, a mile long by half a mile wide, had various names in Welsh, but Ynys Enlli, or Island of Currents, as many a sailor and pilgrim will testify, is the most appropriate. Bardsey (a Norse name) was a refuge for monks escaping massacre by the Saxons and has been a place of pilgrimage since the sixth century, becoming so popular that many of the Welsh bishops had their

Bardsey Island

bodies transported and buried there. Little remains of the priory and the later flourishing community, but it is still a place surrounded by myths, mists and legends. Now it is an important centre for the study of birds and is owned by the Bardsey Island Trust.

Braich y Pwll, the headland opposite Bardsey Island, is a fine windswept spot owned by the National Trust. It is a superb place to appreciate the beauty and setting of the island with only the birds for company. It is the most westerly point of Wales and covers 122 acres, including Mynydd Gwyddel and Mynydd Mawr. Pilgrims embarked here for Bardsey — there was once a chapel here (St Mary's) and it is still possible to find St Mary's Well, although great care should be taken. A short way north there are walks on the common land of Mynydd Anelog, with fine views across to Bardsey and to Aberdaron Bay.

L
*
†††

Northwards the cliff scenery is magnificent and there are many fine walks, broken only by the fine coves of Porth Oer and Porth Golmon. The former is more commonly known as Whistling Sands for the remarkable little squeak given off as one walks on it or runs

BEACHES ON THE NORTHERN SIDE OF THE LLEYN PENINSULA

Whistling Sands (Porth Oer)
Beautiful bay with safe bathing and unique sands that whistle as you walk across them.

Porth Iago
Approached along farm track. Delightful cove, worth finding, a good day out for the whole family.

Porth Golmon (Penllech Beach)
Long stretch of sand with rocks and cliff walks, caves, fishing and good bathing. Interesting church in the village of Llangwnnadl.

Tudweiliog
Pleasant beach with fine sands, fairly small but private. Lovely walks along the coast.

Edern
Safe bathing, good fishing and boats for hire, power and row boats.

Nefyn and Morfa Nefyn
Excellent beaches on wide sandy bays. Popular resorts with bathing, boating and fishing. Golf course on headland. The small village of Porth Dinllaen (along beach or walk over golf course) is well worth a visit, has a pub and a lifeboat station.

one's hands through the dry sand. Apparently the quartz grains of the sand are rounded and of uniform size, and when moved, produces a note of uniform pitch. At Porth Golmon it used to be possible to see cows walking down to and along the Penllech Beach at low tide, returning again to their grazing land before the sea came up again, but this unusual practice seems now to have ceased! Near Porth Oer is Carreg Hall, once the ancient house of Welsh chieftains, but now engaged in the peaceful pursuit of serving afternoon teas.

From this section of coast the most obvious feature when looking inland is the conical hill which thrusts its way upwards. This is Carn Fadron (1,217 ft) equidistant between the north and south shores, and the views from its summit are excellent. The hill has innumerable ancient trackways with much evidence of Iron Age settlement, and its exploration provides a pleasant alternative to

L
$1/_2$-2h
**
†††

Porth Golmon

lounging on the beach.

Near Porth Golmon is the village of **Llangwnnadl**, with its unusual church in a wooded valley running down to the sea. Founded in AD540 it boasts three naves and three altars. On the south wall is the tombstone of the patron saint (St Gwynhoedl) which is thought to date from about AD600. The chalice and paten have been in continuous use since 1574.

Nefyn and **Morfa Nefyn** are the most popular holiday centres along this coast. They both have fine sheltered beaches, ideal for boating and bathing, and, like most of the beaches on the peninsula, have superb views of the mountains, in this case Yr Eifl or The Rivals. Lacking pleasure parks and sideshows, these villages are ideal for quiet family holidays, with many guest houses and hotels and with caravan sites nearby.

Nefyn is the larger of the two and was once a major resting point for the pilgrims to Bardsey Island. **Porth Dinllaen** is a fine natural harbour and its small community can be reached only by a walk along the beach or across the golf course from Morfa Nefyn. It is a

PLACES OF INTEREST NEAR NEFYN

Tre'r-Ceiri
By the footpath, leave the B4417 at top of the hill between Llithfaen and Llanaelhaearn north of Nefyn. Britain's oldest walled village. Built on the crown of a hill. Remains of 250 or so stone huts surrounded by several walls. Built about 3,000-4,000 years ago. Worth the effort of seeing.

Nant Gwrtheyrn
Approach only on foot, about $^3/_4$ mile from car park. Turn off in centre of village of Llithfaen towards the sea, off B4417, 5 miles north of Nefyn. Accessible old quarrying village in ancient Vortigerns Valley, on sea side of Yr Eifl. An idyllic spot with small beach. Being renovated as a centre for Welsh studies.

delightful collection of beach cottages, mostly holiday homes, and a pub. A gentle stroll at low level around the headland takes one to the lifeboat station and a small sandy beach.

Nefyn, and more particularly Porth Dinllaen, was suggested during the early nineteenth century as an alternative to Holyhead as the major port to Ireland. The defeat of the motion by one vote in parliament, saved this beautiful stretch of coast for all to enjoy. North along the beach from Nefyn is Bird Rock, a craggy headland appropriately named for the many different species found there.

Continuing along the coast road from Nefyn, the ancient church of St Beuno at **Pistyll** is worth a visit. The corner stone at the eastern end of the north wall is one of only three known to exist. There is a lepers' window on the north side of the chancel and a saint is buried beneath the altar, possibly St Beuno himself. A mural on the north wall is in red ochre and represents the crucifixion, while high on the wall by the altar window is the date 1050 cut into the stone.

Towering above this stretch of coastland and visible from almost anywhere on Lleyn is Yr Eifl, anglicised to 'The Rivals' but meaning The Forks, because of its three peaks. The highest (1,849ft) is flanked on the seaward side by a much quarried summit (1,458ft), and on the inland side by the third peak (1,591ft), surmounted by the

The Nefyn coast looking towards Yr Eifl (The Rivals)

---

 ruins of the Iron Age hillfort village of Tre'r Ceiri. This site, reached by a steep path from a stile on the Llanaelhaearn road, has the best preserved and most extensive collection of walled huts in the country. What a superb situation for a village. The site covers about five acres of the hill top. Surrounded by several defensive walls which vary in thickness from 7ft to 11ft (the inner one still has much of its parapet), it contains the remains of about fifty huts. Though never properly excavated, and unfortunately not under any obvious protection, it is well worth making the effort to see, but on account of lack of care by visitors, it has over the last few years shown a visible deterioration. A Bronze Age cairn of an earlier date can be seen at its north-eastern point.

From this site the summit of Yr Eifl is reached by an easy path which leads from the south end of Tre'r Ceiri down to a shallow valley and up to the highest peak on the Lleyn. The views are extensive — note down at the foot of the mountain perched almost on the edge of the sea a small village in a dark valley. This is **Nant Gwrtheyrn**, a tiny hamlet once dependent on quarrying, which can

PLACES OF INTEREST ON THE LLEYN PENINSULA'S NORTHERN COAST

Clynnog Fawr Church
On A499 south of Caernarfon.
One of the first churches in
Wales, dedicated to St Beuno.
The rebuilt church stands on the
site of an ancient monastery.
Contains many old relics. Close
to the church is an old burial
site, interesting because the
capstone is carved with
hundreds of cups and rings.

Dinas Dinlle
Off A499, towards Llandwrog
about 5 miles south of Caernarfon.
Oval mound with ramparts and
ditch, an ancient defensive spot
used by British and Romans.

Fort Belan
Eighteenth-century fort with
cannons, maritime museum and
old forge. Tea rooms and gift
shop with pottery. Train rides,
horse rides and even plane rides
above the mountains of
Snowdonia. Something for
everyone. As above but
continue past mound to
aerodrome and headland.

Museum of Old Welsh County Life
Tai'n Lon, Clynnog Fawr, 10
miles south of Caernarfon.
Housed in seventeenth-century
corn mill.

can be reached only by foot down a steep and winding road, There
is a convenient car park at the end of the road leading seawards
from the crossroads in Llithfaen. The descent from the car park on
foot for about a mile brings one to a village of utter peace and quiet
without motor cars. The village is simply two lines of cottages set
around a square and the inevitable chapel. After lying in ruins for
many years the cottages are now being renovated to provide a
centre for Welsh language studies. Below is a fine stretch of sandy
beach.

L
2h
*
†††

The climb back to the car park is a reminder of the plight of the
earlier inhabitants and their weekly visit to the shops. The valley is
steep-sided and sometimes sombre, the reason perhaps for its
other name, Vortigern's Valley. Legend has it that Vortigern, one
time British King, took refuge here before being struck down by

heavenly fire.

The northern side of the hills is less interesting on account of extensive quarrying around Trefor. On the road to Caernarfon the church of **Clynnog Fawr** is worthy of interest. Founded by St Beuno in AD616, it is one of the mother churches of Wales. Until the Dissolution it was a monastery, but the present church dates only from the sixteenth century. It contains many relics of the early saint and he is said to be buried there. Nearby is a much older burial site. Close to the shore and just west of the church is an ancient burial chamber with a cap stone about 6ft high by 8ft long and 5ft wide carved with hundreds of cups or depressions.

The coast continues northwards towards the Menai Straits with an ancient site, and a much more recent one to visit. Taking the road to Llandwrog and to the tip of the Straits you pass the conspicuous Iron Age fort of Dinas Dinlle. It is roughly oval with two ramparts and a ditch, and was probably also used by the Romans. Further on, at the very tip of the headland, is the eighteenth-century Fort Belan, built by Thomas Wynne (Lord Newborough) and garrisoned by a force of 400 men which he raised and equipped at his own expense. It was intended to defend Caernarfon from the French during the Napoleonic wars and as such it was a magnanimous gesture that nearly broke him. Today the fort is one of the area's newest attractions. Besides the building and many of the original features, it has a mini-railway, a pottery, a café and a gift shop. There is something for the whole family — even a light aeroplane for trips over the area and mountains.

Caernarfon is the starting and finishing point for many journeys. To the south the peninsula stretches its arm lazily towards Ireland, its coastline one of the finest in Europe.

6

ANGLESEY

Anglesey is the largest island off the coast of Wales and England. Although separated only by the Menai Straits, which vary from several hundred yards to several miles in width, it retains all the character of an island. The climate is generally milder and drier than that of the mainland nearby, making it ideal for seaside holidays. There are many sandy beaches easily accessible for swimming or boating.

Many visitors to the island will be aware of its prehistoric connections with the Druids and Celtic Christianity, for legend and fact about the past are inextricably mixed. Perhaps like modern visitors the early settlers found the climate more amenable than the mainland and the nearby mountains. There is much evidence of early man's use of the land, and visitors are today welcomed to the island by the sign 'Mon, Mam Cymru — Anglesey, Mother of Wales'. This title comes from the island's early fertility and farming habits. It was always a major supplier of grain to the rest of Wales, for it was said that more grain was grown in Anglesey, the smallest county, than in the rest of the country. Today many of the fields are only pastureland.

Compared with the nearby mountains of Snowdonia, the island is flat, the highest point being just over 500ft above sea level. Geographically there are some fine examples of ancient rocks

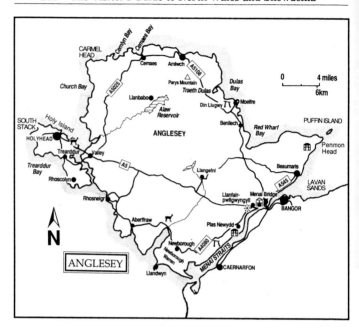

including Pre-Cambrian sandstone and limestone that come to the surface at several places. The main attraction, however, is its coastline, with its sandy beaches and quiet coves.

The Menai Straits, though narrow, are notorious for the tides that race through them and which have made the crossing until recently dangerous and fraught with difficulty. There were at one time seven ferries across the Straits all greatly overcharging for the short trip. The most common route was on foot across the Lavan Sands near Bangor and then by ferry across the remaining water to Beaumaris (Biwmares). Cattle going to market were forced to swim across, urged on by the drovers in the boats, but losses were high and life hazardous for all travellers.

 Today's visitor is more fortunate, for in 1826 Thomas Telford completed his remarkable suspension bridge as part of the London to Holyhead (Caergybi) road. Faced with the problem of bridging the Straits but allowing room for the tall fully rigged sailing ships to

Menai Straits from Port Dinorwig

Telford's road bridge over the Menai Straits

143

The rebuilt Britannia Bridge, which now carries both road and rail

pass underneath, he built the world's second chain suspension bridge. The towers of locally quarried limestone held the massive chains which were anchored into the solid rock at each end, with the road suspended below on wrought iron rods. For the first time it became possible to cross to and from the mainland with dry feet for a small toll charge, and stage coaches and mail coaches made the bridge an instant success. The graceful lines of the bridge were unfortunately not designed for twentieth-century loads and in 1936 major strengthening took place. Though not detracting from the appearance of the bridge, it has enabled it to cope with today's traffic.

The neighbouring Britannia Bridge had an equally illustrious past. Another great engineer, Robert Stephenson, built the railway between London and Holyhead for the Irish ferry. Faced also with the problem of sailing ships he solved it by constructing two parallel wrought-iron tubes high above the water between three towers, at the time a unique solution. Opened in 1850 and in continuous use until 1970, when it was accidentally destroyed by fire, it was a tribute to the foresight of the Victorian engineers. The re-modelled Britannia Bridge has one level for trains and an upper level for road traffic and though perhaps not as graceful as the earlier bridge it has at least lightened the load on Telford's Suspension Bridge and eased the traffic-flow problem in summer. Much of Stephenson's original work remains incorporated in the new bridge.

The first Marquess of Anglesey greets all visitors to the island as they cross the Straits. From high on his limestone column he surveys his domain and casts an approving eye over the two bridges. Inside there are steps up to a balustrade surrounding the top. It provides a dizzy vantage point from which to survey the island, the Straits and the mountains of Snowdonia, but it is not for the acrophobic. Unfortunately the marquess never saw the statue, for he died at the age of 86, five years before it was completed. He rose to fame as the Duke of Wellington's second in command at the Battle of Waterloo. As Lord Paget, he had been accompanying the duke from the battlefield when a cannon ball smashed his leg. 'By God, sir, I've lost my leg' he shouted to the Duke. 'By God, sir, so you have' replied Wellington, and resumed surveying the retreating French. For his bravery at that battle he was created the First

The railway station sign at Llanfair PG

Board showing the scale of charges payable at the Llanfair PG toll house

Telford's octagonal toll house at Llanfair PG on the London to Holyhead road

Plas Newydd on the shores of the Menai Straits

The chambered cairn of Bryn-Celli-Ddu

PLACES OF INTEREST AROUND MENAI

Llanfairpwllgwyngyllogerych-wyrndrobwllllantysiliogo-gogoch
Village with the world's longest place name, also the longest platform ticket in the world, available at the railway station souvenir shop. Officially known as Llanfair PG.

Marquess of Anglesey's Column
90ft tall with statue on top commemorating the First Marquess, Lord Paget. Views from platform of mountains and Menai Straits are superb.

Plas Newydd
Off A4080 two miles from Llanfair PG.
Home of Marquess of Anglesey, on edge of Menai Straits, with many fine pictures, some by Rex Whistler, and also mementoes of the Battle of Waterloo. Beautiful grounds.

Toll House, Llanfair PG
On A5 at start of village. Last to operate, until 1895, still displays tolls.

Plas Goch Leisure Park
On side of Menai Straits next door to Plas Newydd.
Caravan site, swimming pool, picnic areas and mini golf. Many other attractions including restaurant and disco in evening.

Bryn-Celli-Ddu
1$\frac{1}{2}$ miles north of A4080 to Llanddaniel Fab, walk up farm track.
Best preserved burial mound with huge stones and passage. Probably early Bronze Age.

Brynsiencyn
There are many ancient sites in the fields around the village including burial chambers and earthworks.

Brynsiencyn Pottery
In centre of the village off A4080.

Anglesey Sea Zoo
Brynsiencyn
Aquarium with displays of marine animals from Britain's coast.

Marquess of Anglesey. With his family he lived at Plas Newydd just a mile away and despite his wooden leg he continued to have a successful career in government.

The A5 crosses the two bridges and runs by the marquess' feet.

It then turns inland to cross the island, and very soon arrives at probably the most famous village in Anglesey. Known throughout Britain for having the longest name is **Llanfairpwllgwyngyll**, or quite simply Llanfair PG. The name was further extended to a total of fifty-eight letters by a local wit at the end of the last century, presumably for the benefit of tourists and became Llanfairpwllgwyngyllogerychwyrndrobwllllantysiliogogogoch. The tiny station has the doubtful distinction of issuing the longest platform ticket in the world and probably also having the longest sign.

By the side of the road on the way into the village is an octagonal toll house designed by Telford. It was the last toll house to operate in Wales, finally opening its gates in 1895, and it still bears the sign stating the tolls. This attractive building is a tribute to the genius of the engineer who did everything so well.

The A5 continues its journey to its destination at Holyhead almost bisecting the island in the process. It is not a particularly exciting drive, for the scenery is fairly plain and the road seems to stretch endlessly in front. Unless one is dashing to the ferry to Ireland or off to climb the sea cliffs on Holy Island it is infinitely more pleasant to take the less busy roads that follow the coast.

It is convenient to start from the Anglesey Column and take the A4080 which runs parallel with the Menai Straits. After about a mile is the house of **Plas Newydd** between the road and the Straits. One may take the opportunity to relax in the tranquil gardens and take in the magnificent views across the mountains of Snowdonia. Plas Newydd was the home of the First Marquess of Anglesey, and it now has a small museum devoted to his military career with some mementoes of Waterloo. It was built in the eighteenth century by James Wyatt, and there are some fine rooms, furniture and por-traits, as well as sketches, letters and more important works by Rex Whistler including his largest wall painting. This huge mural is well worth stopping to examine in detail. Fortunately a guide is nearby to explain its many features and the actual people who are featured on it. Perhaps one of its most memorable features is the perspec-tive. Whichever end of this long room you happen to be at, the painted flagstones above the sea wall appear to be laid towards you! Outside, the lawns slope down to the sea wall. During the

The wide sweep of Newborough Warren's sandy beach

Anglesey Sea Zoo, Brynsiencyn

summer a boat service from the quay at Caernarfon offers trips along the straits to the house, a most unusual approach.

Nearby is the Plas Goch Leisure Park, which seems to have something for everybody — a heated outdoor swimming pool, play and picnic areas, bars, cafés and a caravan park. All this is situated in the 200 acres of parkland surrounding the fifteenth-century Manor House. With a direct frontage on to the Straits it is also well equipped for watersports.

On the opposite side of the road to Plas Goch, and up a short lane, is the chambered cairn of Bryn-Celli-Ddu. This is the best preserved of all the burial chambers on Anglesey and is easily accessible on foot from the road. Originally 160ft in diameter and covering the whole of the area inside the fenced enclosure, little was found when it was excavated in 1928. The stone chamber dates from about 2000BC but the covering mound is a modern weather protection. From the car park is a gateway to the farm and it is a short walk along the lane to the cairn.

This southern corner of the island has many similar burial chambers, though none quite as well preserved as Bryn-Celli-Ddu. It does indicate that this was probably the most inhabited part of the island in ancient times. The sea is nearby, the land is flat and it was not as tree-covered as elsewhere. Stories of Druids are well known and give Anglesey a reputation it has never quite lived down. They were not the fearsome people we have come to expect, but the religious leaders of a particular sect, living on the island to escape persecution by the Romans. The burial chambers and cairns in the area probably even pre-date the Druids and are not, as many people imagine, the sacrificial altars of these notorious priests. Though there is in fact very little evidence of their religious monuments, it is known that this particular corner of the island was their headquarters in the early centuries after Christ.

On the edge of the Menai Straits, almost opposite Caernarfon, is the Anglesy Sea Zoo. This marine aquarium has examples of sea life from all round Britain's coast, including some species which are now quite scarce.

No love was lost between the Romans and Druids, and after a fearsome battle on the very edge of the Straits the Romans succeeded in invading the island. They destroyed everything connected with the religion and subdued the people. It was not until several centuries after the withdrawal of the Romans that Anglesey re-established itself as a religious centre with the coming of Christianity.

Newborough, formerly Rhosyr, was built to house the people displaced by Edward I during the construction of Beaumaris Castle. The area beyond the village towards the sea, is not one of the busiest parts of the island but it is certainly one of the nicest. From the centre of the village a narrow road goes out to the forest behind the town. There is a charge to enter the forest by road, which gives access to one of the finest beaches in North Wales, with car parks and picnic spots.

The forest is one vast nature reserve covering the sand dunes and salt marshes behind the sea shore. Known as Newborough Warren for the number of rabbits which used to live there — 80,000 were trapped annually — the dunes cover the old village of Rhosyr and its field system. It is hoped that the trees and grasses recently

PLACES OF INTEREST ON THE SOUTHERN SIDE OF ANGLESEY

Newborough Warren and Malltraeth Sands
Superb beach surrounded by forest with many forest trails and picnic spots. Access to car park behind dunes (small toll).

Llanddwyn
Off A4080 in Newborough village. Approach across beach from Newborough Warren. A peninsula of Pre-Cambrian rock, now a nature reserve, with old cottages, lifeboat station and lighthouse. A grand spot for views of the hills across the bay.

Aberffraw
Sandy beach with island church of St Cwfan on site of early Celtic church.

Glantraeth Zoo Garden
Off B4422 between Newborough and Aberffraw. Collection of small animals in private grounds. Ideal for children, also farm museum and restaurant.

Rhosneigr
Sandy beaches ideal for bathing and boating. Popular resort with many areas for birdwatching around the village.

Valley Airfield
Off A5 before crossing to Holy Island. Car park near RAF aerodrome for 'plane spotters'. Jet trainers and helicopters can be seen coming and going frequently.

planted will stabilise the drifting sands. There are several paths and nature trails through the reserve and visitors should stay on the marked paths. An information leaflet is available on the site.

Besides the extensive forests there is a huge beach and foreshore with fine golden sands. It is close to the car park and is never crowded, stretching for several miles in each direction. It is a short walk across the beach to **Llanddwyn Island**, a promontory connected to the mainland by a narrow strip of rock. The island is a nature reserve criss-crossed by easily followed footpaths. Many wild flowers grow in the grass and undergrowth; visitors are asked to stay on the paths. Birds can be seen nesting around the island's cliffs, and there are superb views of the mainland hills.

On the tip of the island is a lighthouse and lifeboat station above a small bay. The lifeboatmen's cottages have been renovated as a visitor centre where there are leaflets giving an outline of the flora and fauna in the area. The adjacent cottages are furnished in original style giving a glimpse of eighteenth-century life there. There are several more miles of beach with Malltraeth sands to the north of the island, all accessible from the car park. The area is highly recommended for a fascinating day out.

Until the building of an embankment connecting Newborough with Malltraeth the estuary of the Afon Cefni almost cut the island in half. Now the low lying land is being turned into pastureland, with the estuary on the seaward side of the embankment silting up to create even more expanses of sand at low tide, teeming with wild fowl and waders.

Aberffraw, just beyond Newborough, was for many centuries the capital of Gwynedd and home of the Welsh Princes. Nothing remains today of their palaces, though a Norman arch in the church of St Beuno is traditionally said to have been built by them. The village, a busy port before the coming of the railways, is now a popular holiday centre with some fine beaches and rocky headlands. Accessible at low tide is the tiny church of St Cwyfan, built on a small island. It is thought to have been founded originally in the seventh century but was extensively rebuilt in 1893.

The bays to the north were the haunt of the eighteenth-century wreckers who lured ships on to the nearby rocks. Today they are popular with yachtsmen and weekend sailors, and some of them are particularly suitable for canoe surfing. **Rhosneigr** stands be- tween two beautiful bays, both excellent for swimming and water sports. It was a popular Edwardian resort, and has remained an ideal family holiday town. The extensive area of gorse-covered dunes just to the north is Tywyn Trewan Common, a paradise for bird watchers and botanists.

For those who prefer to watch the creations of modern technology the nearby RAF aerodrome at **Valley** is the home of the RAF advanced jet flying school and the regional centre for the air/sea rescue service. Aircraft and helicopters are coming and going all day long, many on training flights, and there is a car park for plane spotters. The airfield was originally built in 1941 as a terminal for transatlantic crossings for the USAF. During its construction a large cache of bronze weapons and other implements was found in a

The walls of the Roman fort at Holyhead

lake. Known as the Llyn Cerrig Bach hoard, it is now in the National Museum of Wales and is thought to have been votive offerings for Iron Age religious ceremonies.

Across the bay is **Holy Island (Ynys Gybi)**, separated by a narrow strip of water from the main island, and for many centuries the religious centre of Anglesey. Thought to have been the religious stronghold of the Druids, it was settled in the sixth century by St Cybi who built a small church within the remains of the Roman fort at Holyhead. He was a formidable character who travelled the whole of Anglesey converting the people. There is still a church dedicated to him within the walls of the Roman fort at Holyhead, but it is a much more recent building with some fine carved stonework. Roman stonework is clearly seen in the walls of the churchyard. The town of Holyhead is still known in Welsh as Caergybi, Gybi's fortress.

Holyhead is a bustling town, which has grown to be the largest in Anglesey. It is basically a seaport servicing the busy Irish ferry boats and the developing trade in container ships. The town

*South Stack
Lighthouse,
Holy Island*

surrounds the harbour and is gradually spreading up the slopes of
Holyhead mountain. Holyhead is also developing as a yachting
centre with a pleasant shingle beach and safe mooring, protected
by a long breakwater. A promenade, running along its full length,
makes it also extremely popular for sea fishermen.

It has been difficult to avoid the busy A5 trunk road as it carves
its way so impressively through the heart of North Wales, particularly as several of the bridges are so significant in the development
of the area and are impressive features in their own right. In Holyhead the road finally reaches its destination and terminates at a triumphal arch on the quayside, just 267 miles from Marble Arch in
London — a triumph of engineering in its time.

Behind the town, Holyhead Mountain rises gently to the low
banks of an ancient hill fort of indeterminate age on its summit.
Much of the headland is a nature reserve controlled by the Royal

PLACES OF INTEREST ON HOLY ISLAND

Beaches

Holyhead
Sand and shingle beach inside harbour breakwater (1$\frac{1}{2}$ mile long).

Trearddur Bay
Fine sands with rocky outcrops, ideal for bathing and many water sports.

Rhoscolyn
Sandy beaches with good sheltered bathing. Fine cliff walks.

Silver Bay
Sandy beach near mouth of channel between the two islands.

Holyhead (Caergybi)

Roman walls surrounding church of St Gybi, near town centre. Triumphal arch to celebrate completion of A5 and visit of George IV. Busy port for Irish ferries protected by 1$\frac{1}{2}$ mile breakwater with road along. Ideal for fishing.

South Stack Lighthouse

Steps down give magnificent views of cliffs with nesting birds and rock climbers. Lighthouse open in afternoons during summer.

Ellen's Tower

Bird observatory overlooking South Stack Lighthouse and cliffs, just below the car park for the lighthouse. All the headland is owned by the RSPB. Care should be taken when walking in the area.

Holyhead Mountain Hut Circles

By road to South Stack. Remains of an extensive settlement of second-fourth centuries. Circular and square huts, once thatched. Some have central hearths and upright slabs showing positions of beds and seats.

Feilw Standing Stones

Penrhos, 1$\frac{3}{4}$ mile south-west of Holyhead.
Two stones believed to be the remains of a larger circle. There are several other standing stones on the island for those interested in these antiquities.

Penrhos

Off A5 south of Holyhead. Nature reserve with woodlands and sea birds. Nature trails.

 Society for the Protection of Birds. The steep cliffs and hillsides are a favourite nesting place for many seabirds including puffins, guillemots, gulls and razorbills. During June and July the rare auk

The cliffs at North Stack, Holy Island

may also be seen there. Perhaps the best place to observe the birds is from the area around South Stack Lighthouse.

In a magnificent setting the lighthouse has a true 'Land's End' feel about it. Surrounded by steep cliffs, it can be approached down 379 steps from a car park. They are the best way to see the superb cliff faces around the lighthouse and observe the birds. The rocks offer some of the hardest climbing in Wales for many climbers from the mainland; except in the nesting season they vie with the seabirds for every little ledge and handhold. The lighthouse is on a small island at the bottom of the cliffs, approached across a small suspension bridge. It is open to the public each afternoon during the L summer. For the statistically minded the lighthouse is automatic, 1h 91ft high and 197ft above high water. Built in 1808 by David Alex- †††† ander, who also built Dartmoor Prison, it is probably the most visited lighthouse in Britain.

Just below the car park and perched on the very edge of the cliffs is a squat square building that was for many years an ugly ruin. Known as Ellin's Tower, it was built in 1868 by the Rt Hon Owen

Stanley (MP for Penrhos) as a place to enjoy the view. Recently it has been converted by the Royal Society for the Protection of Birds into an observatory for bird watchers, for there are fine views of the cliffs. It provides a welcome refuge from the wind for ornithologists and other visitors, who are welcomed.

The whole of the South Stack area is full of interest. Alongside the approach road to the lighthouse is a fine collection of hut circles. They are the remains of twenty huts of various shapes and sizes believed to be part of a much larger settlement. Easily accessible from the road they give a good idea of how our ancestors lived, showing signs of their sleeping slabs and hearths. Now in the care of the State they perpetuate in the name Cythiau'r Gwyddelod, or Irishmen's Walls, in the belief that they were built by settlers from across the sea, although there is no evidence to substantiate this. Nearby are two large standing stones, which are thought to have been the centre stones of a much larger circle, although they now stand alone. Throughout Holy Island there are many other standing stones and hut circles, perhaps indicating that it was after all the centre of religion long before Christianity arrived.

To the south of Holyhead there are several popular holiday resorts, particularly **Trearddur Bay** which sits astride the pre-Telford road to the island. It has several fine beaches with golden sands and rocky outcrops just offshore, making it popular with skin divers and water skiers, though it can be windy. **Rhoscolyn**, on the southern tip, equally popular for water sports, is more sheltered from the wind. From the village there are some fine cliff-top walks particularly to the well of St Gwenfaen which is reputed to be able to cure mental illness. The nearby cliffs have rock formations showing the bending and folding which took place during the earth's formation.

Back on Anglesey the coast to the north with its small bays and rocky coves is very reminiscent of Cornwall. All the beaches give good views across the bay to Holy Island and Holyhead. **Church Bay** is perhaps the most visited beach on that stretch of coast. This north-west corner of the island is dominated by the hill of Mynydd y Garn, which, like any hill surrounded by flat land, appears much higher than it actually is. A road runs very close to the top leaving but a short walk to the gorse-topped summit. The views are of the

BEACHES AND PLACES OF INTEREST ALONG THE NORTH COAST OF ANGLESEY

Church Bay
Partly sand with rocky outcrops, good views across to Holy Island and Holyhead. Fine cliff walks.

Carmel Head
Rocky coves with good cliff walks.

Cemlyn Bay
Steep shelving pebble beach, now a bird sanctuary.

Cemaes Bay
Fine harbour and sandy bay. Good swimming and cliff walks to Llanbadrig and church. Overlooked by Wylfa Nuclear Power Station, which is open to visitors in summer.

Bull Bay
Rocky cove with sheltered bathing and good walks.

Amlwch
Small narrow harbour, old port for nearby copper mines of Parys Mountain. Swimming pool in town.

Parys Mountain
Eighteenth-century copper mines, now a mountain of waste. Some interesting coloured rocks to be seen and industrial archaeology remains, but care must be taken.

Llyn Alaw
Off B5112 at Llanerchymedd. Visitor centre and fishing on reservoir.

nearby coast, Carmel Head and the Wylfa Power Station. Off Carmel Head, The Skerries can be seen, a small group of islets used by breeding birds and seals. The lighthouse on The Skerries has been there since the eighteenth century and was one of the early examples that extracted a toll from every passing ship.

East of the headland the cliffs seem to get wilder until **Cemlyn Bay** is reached. The sheltered beach, once the haunt of pirates, is now a bird sanctuary owned by the National Trust. Visitors are requested to take care during the nesting season (April-June) if they use the cliff top walks around the bay and headland. Much of this northern coast, however, is dominated by the massive bulk of the

Parys Mountain   Above: *Remains of the great open-cast copper mine*

Ruins of a mine enginehouse on Parys Mountain

Amlwch harbour

Wylfa Nuclear Power Station. As the power station is in an area of outstanding natural beauty, the Central Electricity Generating Board has provided a nature trail around the headland. There is also an observation tower for looking over the power station and surroundings, while during the summer visitors can tour the site (by appointment).

Several little harbours along the northern coast are worth visiting. The nearest to Wylfa is **Cemaes Bay**; its tiny harbour and pleasant beach are well sheltered from all but the northernmost winds. The cliffs alongside the bay are National Trust property with some pleasant walks, particularly along to Llanbadrig. The church above the cliffs is dedicated to St Patrick and is believed to be on the site of one of the oldest churches in Anglesey. It is said that Patrick was shipwrecked on the little island of Middle Mouse just a short distance from the headland. He established a church here as thanksgiving for his salvation before leaving to convert the people of Ireland.

Amlwch, a little further east, has a fine little harbour, built of unmortared rock placed vertically rather than horizontally. It is small and narrow, owing its fame to the nearby Parys Mountain copper mine. During the heyday of the mine, it became the main port for the export of copper and the remains of the old quays can still be seen. Ships were built at the port after the decline of the copper industry and the remains of the old slipways can be seen. It has now become a major oil port. At the Anglesey Marine Terminal two miles offshore, crude oil tankers of more than 500,000 tons can moor and discharge their cargo. It is pumped directly ashore and through an underground pipeline to Stanlow, seventy-eight miles away in Cheshire, where it is refined. The harbour has had a new lease of life servicing the terminal and has been expanded.

Inland from Amlwch are the scarred remains of **Parys Mountain**. Once the biggest open-cast copper mine in the world, it produced 80,000 tons of ore per year until the early nineteenth century. In the eighteenth century the output was so great as almost to cause the collapse of the whole of Cornwall's great copper mining industry. Visitors must beware of the dangerous shafts and waste heaps around the scattered workings. Efforts are being made to work the mine again, and to show visitors life and conditions in its heyday.

Further inland, behind the mountain, is Llyn Alaw, a fairly new reservoir much favoured by trout fishermen. The church at nearby **Llanbabo** has three grotesque carved faces above the door, while inside is a finely carved slab believed to date from the fourteenth century. There are also several standing stones and burial mounds around the lake. One in particular, known as Bedd Branwen (Branwen's grave), is traditionally the burying place of Branwen mentioned in the Welsh folk legends *The Mabinogion*.

The eastern side of the island is extremely popular for family holidays. Most of the beaches are well sheltered, with good stretches of fine golden sands and safe bathing. Behind, the countryside is more rolling than elsewhere, with trees more noticeable than on the windy north and west coasts.

Traeth Dulas to the north is a quiet estuary and land-locked bay. Quite out of place are the remains of the old brickworks established in the heyday of Parys Mountain, presumably to cash in on the lucrative building projects. The nearby beaches of Traeth Lligwy are

BEACHES AND PLACES OF INTEREST ON THE EASTERN COAST OF ANGLESEY

Traeth Dulas
Land-locked bay with sandy beach. Also remains of old brickworks from heyday of nearby Parys Mountain.

Traeth Lligwy
Sandy beach backed by dunes and fields. Nearby is Iron Age village of Din Lligwy, a short walk across fields to walled village with remains of hut circles, a pleasant stroll. Also Capel Lligwy, a church standing above headland. Nearby is a Neolithic (New Stone Age) burial chamber with massive capstone. All are just by the road $1/2$ mile north of Llanallgo church.

Moelfre
Boat hire, sailing and water skiing. Pebble beach.

Benllech
Long sandy beach, with donkey rides, deckchairs and cafés. Very popular.

Red Wharf Bay (Traeth Coch)
Wide bay with long walk to the sea when tide is out. Good sand and good bathing at high tide.

excellent, backed by sand dunes.

On the approach roads to the beaches overlooking the bay are several antiquities well worth visiting. They are all signposted from the main road and all can be seen at any time with only a short easy walk. The largest is Din Lligwy, probably the fourth-century fortified residence of a native chieftain. Now surrounded by woods it is a fine example, with much of the floor plan and walls evident. On the same walk is Capel Lligwy, a church of obscure origin but in a superb situation. Just a short distance along the road is the Lligwy Burial Chamber, with an impressive cap stone of solid limestone about 15ft square and 3ft thick, supported on a ring of upright rock 'posts'. It was probably erected in the early Bronze Age, about 2,000BC.

Moelfre, out on the headland, has boats for hire, and, a pebbly beach which is good for water skiing and sailing. The lifeboat station has been involved in many famous disasters; perhaps the best

Penmon Priory and dovecote

known is the *Royal Charter* which went down nearby with the loss
of 452 lives in 1859. To the south, the beaches of **Benllech** and **Red
Wharf Bay** are the most popular on the island. They are long and
sandy, and at low tide Red Wharf Bay is an extensive estuary.
Benllech has donkey rides, deck chairs and sea front cafés. There
are several caravan sites along this section of coast.

Stretching out towards the main land is **Penmon Head**, with
Puffin Island just offshore. Although the coast is scarred by the
remains of old limestone quarries, used during the building of both
Telford's and Stephenson's bridges across the Menai Straits, the
headland is a pretty spot. It can be approached through Penmon
Priory whose remains, mainly eleventh century, are adjacent to the
road and there is a fine dovecote. Much of the priory is still in use,
the abbot's house is still inhabited and the attached church still a
parish church. Just behind the buildings is the well of St Seiriol, an
early Celtic saint active on the island at the same time as St Cybi.
Around the well are a few small buildings and the remains of an oval
hut, possibly the early saint's cell.

For a small toll you can drive to the coastguard station and café

Beaumaris Castle, surrounded by its moat

at Trwyn Du or Black Point just opposite **Puffin Island**. It is a grand spot and with the mournful toll of the bell on the lighthouse one can easily conjure up thoughts of shipwrecks. The island, also known as Priestholme or Ynys Seiriol, once had a small monastery, later

moved to Penmon Priory — and of course many puffins. The bird population declined on account of the popularity of pickled young birds in the early nineteenth century. At the point, there are some

small sandy beaches and excellent views across to the mountains of Snowdonia, particularly the Carneddau. On the south is the entrance to the Menai Straits and across the bay are the Lavan Sands, once the main route to the island.

It was to command this route into Anglesey that Edward I built a castle at **Beaumaris**, almost on the edge of the Straits. It is small compared with its two near neighbours at Conwy and Caernarfon, but around it are the remains of a moat which once connected the castle to the sea. Because of its lowlying situation it does not at first sight seem impressive but it is in fact one of the most complete and best designed castles built during Edward's reign. Despite its solid

PLACES OF INTEREST ALONG THE MENAI STRAITS

Penmon Priory and Dovecote
On road from Beaumaris to
Puffin Island.
Medieval monastery still partly
in use as house and church.
Dovecote is sixteenth century
with room for 1,000 nests. Good
solid stone building with domed
roof.

St Seriol's Well
Penmon
Holy well close to priory with
some stone walls possibly of
the original saint's cell. About
sixth century. Short walk from
priory.

Puffin Island
Along road past Penmon Priory
(small toll).
Just off Black Point (Trwyn Du),
lighthouse with melancholy bell,
coastguard station with café
and pebbly beach. A lonely
spot.

Church of St Tysilio
On island in Menai Straits
accessible by causeway from
Belgian walks.

Tegfryn Art Gallery
Cadnant Road, Menai Bridge.
Exhibitions by Welsh artists.

Belgian Walks
Menai Bridge.
Constructed by Belgian

refugees during World War I as
a promenade. Give good views
of Telford's suspension bridge.

Museum of Childhood
Water Street, Menai Bridge.
Fascinating collection of toys,
games and other things that
have held children's interest
throughout the ages. Suitable
for all ages.

Butterfly Palace (Pili-Palas)
Hundreds of butterflies from all
over the world. Exotic plants,
nature shop and picnic sites at
Menai Bridge.

Beaumaris Castle
Last of Edward I's mighty forts,
once accessible by sea, now
well preserved and not aggres-
sive looking. Children's
playground next to it.

Beaumaris Courthouse
Oldest courthouse in the country
still in use. All the original
furniture and fittings still intact,
very interesting if you are
unfamiliar with such buildings.
Opposite castle.

Beaumaris Jail
Built in 1829 and still as it was,
with treadwheel and cells. All
the work rooms, exercise yards
and punishment blocks are
complete.

defences it has seen little trouble, a short occupation by the Welsh during Owain Glyndwr's uprising in 1404 probably being the high point of its career. Nevertheless it is a charming little castle, with a children's playground against the outside wall.

 Opposite the entrance to the castle is the courthouse built in 1614. Still in its original state and still in use, it is furnished as it was built with the coat of arms of James I over the bench and the public area separated by massive iron bars. Until the last century it was the main Assize Court for the county, but since 1971 it has been only a magistrates' court. It is the oldest courthouse in the country and it is said that the notorious Judge Jefferies once held an Assize here. An equally fascinating place for those unfamiliar with the ways of justice is Beaumaris Jail. Built in 1829, it still has all the cells, the punishment cell and a treadwheel unique in Britain. There is much of interest and one is reminded of the harshness of our early penal system.

The town has several other interesting buildings in its narrow streets, including the Bull's Head Hotel, a favourite with visiting judges and believed to have played host to General Mytton, Cromwell's general during his Anglesey campaign, Dr Johnson and Charles Dickens. The church of St Mary and St Nicholas is almost as old as the castle and has many interesting features. Above the town is the obelisk memorial to the Bulkeley family, once the biggest landowners on the island, whose home at Baron Hill is now an overgrown ruin.

 Beaumaris plays host each August to the Straits Regatta, a major yachting event organised by the Royal Anglesey Yacht Club. The town has something for everyone: bowls, tennis, fishing, many elegant buildings and excellent views.

By comparison, **Menai Bridge** seems a busy little town crouching below Telford's suspension bridge. To suit children of all ages, including grownups, is the Museum of Childhood near the town centre, with some fine displays of toys, games and furniture. The Tegfryn Art Gallery has regular shows by Welsh artists. Along the Belgian Walks, built by refugees during World War I, there are several pleasant walks to Church Island, out in the Straits, which is easily reached by a causeway.

With the building of the two bridges, much of the importance of the towns along the Straits was removed. Holyhead became the biggest and most important town and Llangefni, almost in the centre of the island, took over the role of administrative centre from Beaumaris. **Llangefni** is a bustling market town with wide streets (market day Thursday), situated on the Afon Cefni by which it could once be reached by boat. There are some easy walks in the vicinity of the town. However, most visitors to the island come to see the coastline and the beaches, and will probably spend little time in the interior. There is something for everybody on Anglesey and there is always the probability of warmer weather than on the mainland, so go prepared for a relaxing time.

—— 7 ——
BLAENAU FFESTINIOG, BARMOUTH AND BALA

The area of country bounded on the north by the Lledr Valley and the Vale of Ffestiniog and to the south by Llyn Tegid and the Mawddach Estuary contains some of the best, and at the same time the least known, mountains of Snowdonia. The ranges to the north with fourteen peaks over 3,000ft are well known and well visited, but how many people are aware of the quieter slopes of the Rhinogs, the Arenigs and the surrounding hills?

Visitors to this area, either walking or touring, can expect some pleasant surprises. It is a large area crossed by few roads. The hills and moorlands are high, divided by long valleys bearing the inevitable main road; but the character of the country is such that there are few of these. On the side facing Tremadog Bay are twenty miles of beautiful golden sands with some of the best bathing in North Wales.

It must be said that to gain the most from this compact highland area, you must be prepared to get off the beaten track a little. The area abounds with lakes and reservoirs, some easily accessible, others up tiny minor roads that wander uphill far into the mountains. Walkers will be at an advantage here. The hills are rough and craggy, and with many ancient trackways into and across them, their efforts will be well rewarded. It is a wonderful area to explore, but do be prepared to be adventurous.

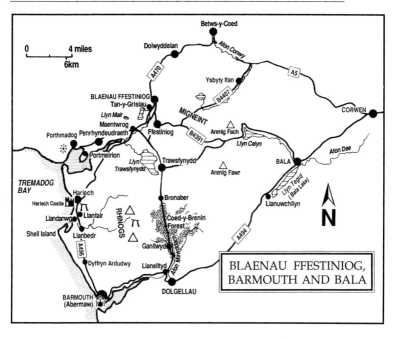

The towns in the area are small, reflecting much that is Welsh — not for them the bright lights and noises, but honest down-to-earth service, and the main language of the area is Welsh.

When the National Park was designated, **Blaenau Ffestiniog**, almost in the centre, was excluded. As an industrial town with huge slate tips towering above it, the grey terraces of houses blending in to give a gloomy view particularly in the rain, it was considered to be a blot on the landscape. Now, thirty years after that decision, the quarries no longer produce slate in any quantity and the once ugly town is ironically a popular centre for visitors. It is the slate they come to see, and slate artefacts they come to buy.

There are many sorts of mining and quarrying in North Wales, but it is slate for which the region is best known: until recently most buildings had a slate roof. Now with clay or concrete roof tiles, and even imitation slates, there is very little slate mined in the area. Several other towns have been dominated by slate, including

View from the Llechwedd Slate Cavern

Llanberis and Bethesda, but in Blaenau Ffestiniog everything is slate. It has been the life and breath of the community for two hundred years, though now most of the quarries are quiet and the drainage pumps switched off.

Slate underlies most of Snowdonia and appears frequently on or near the surface. Where it does appear it can be quarried, but around Blaenau it was found easier to mine it. Many of the seams are forty or fifty feet thick and tilted at an angle of forty-five degrees; so the caverns created when the slate was removed are enormous, large enough to contain an average size house.

Undoubtedly life in the quarry was hard: men, usually all from the same family, worked in small groups. They were paid according to their production, and there was no time for idling: they worked underground by candlelight. One man did the drilling to blast the rock loose, sometimes working high above the ground suspended only by a rope around one thigh. The others would break up and reduce the blocks to more manageable sizes, ready for removal. Outside they would be shaped and dressed as required. Each size

Typical slate mining ruins at Rhosydd, high up in the Moelwyn hills

of roofing slate had its own name: countess, princess, wide lady and many more.

Two mines are open to the public in Blaenau Ffestiniog, on opposite sides of the A470 before it crosses the Crimea Pass to Dolwyddelan. On the north side is Gloddfa Ganol, the largest slate mine in the world, and on the south, the Llechwedd Slate Cavern; both have visitor centres and guided tours down the caverns to experience the miners' conditions. There are shops for souvenirs and one can watch slates being trimmed and cut in the old way. Justifiably, they are both very popular and can be well recommended.

For the walker it is possible to visit many of the older disused mines in the hills surrounding Blaenau though care must be taken and shafts avoided. A short distance from the town is **Tan-y-Grisiau**, a small community surrounded by remnants of its slate-mining past. A steep track rises from the back of the village up to Llyn Cwmorthin and an old chapel; beyond are the barracks and sheds of the old quarries. The path uphill past the chapel continues

M
4-5h
***
††††

PLACES OF INTEREST
AROUND BLAENAU FFESTINIOG

Llechwedd Slate Cavern
Trips inside the slate caverns by tram, and to the deeper caverns by special railway. Demonstrations of slate working and photos of life in quarries. Slide and photographic displays.

Gloddfa Ganol
Displays of massive machinery used in the slate industry and visits to the mines wearing helmets and miners' lamps. Collection of old steam engines.

Ffestiniog Power Station
First pumped storage scheme in Britain. Tours of the power station and the top lake are available. Book at the information centre at Tan-y-Grisiau.

to the old Rhosydd mines, the highest in Wales. It is easy to imagine the hardships of the miner as he walked this path to work at the beginning of each week. Here all the slate was mined, and the tunnels (or 'adits' as they are known) stretch up and through the hillside.

This is the back of Moelwyn Mawr and a walk up the old inclines or the old tracks through the Rhosydd quarry leads to two great holes from which the slate has been extracted. Just behind these and over the shoulder is a terraced track which can be followed easily around the hillside to the south to above Llyn Stwlan, the top lake of a pump storage scheme. From there a road leads back downhill to Tan-y-Grisiau. The lower reservoir is a favourite place for trout fishermen. The adjacent power station can be visited by appointment, and there is a visitors' information centre, open daily during the season.

The Festiniog Railway, one of the 'Great Little Trains of Wales', runs between Blaenau Ffestiniog and Porthmadog. Operated now mainly by volunteers, this narrow gauge railway was originally built to carry the slate from the mines in Blaenau to the quay at Porthmadog. Now it provides a regular passenger service for most of the year. The scenery en route is superb, as the track drops from

The Festiniog Railway as it climbs towards Blaenau Ffestiniog

the hills down the beautiful Vale of Ffestiniog before skirting the estuary of Traeth Mawr and crossing the Cob (or embankment) to Porthmadog. It is more usual to catch the train at Porthmadog and do the return journey to and from the terminus near Blaenau Ffestiniog. The little engines are original and excellently maintained. A connecting bus runs up to the slate quarries for visitors. (See also chapter 5, pages 124-5).

Near neighbour to Blaenau Ffestiniog is **Ffestiniog**, a quiet little

Llyn Mair behind Plas Tan-y-Bwlch,
the Snowdonia National Park Study Centre

village, standing at the head of the valley to which it gives its name and with superb views of the surrounding mountains. Below, the Vale of Ffestiniog is justifiably said to be the most beautiful in North Wales. The steep sided slopes are covered in many places with the original oakwoods that once covered most of Wales. The Afon Dwyryd meanders lazily along the valley bottom to an ancient stone bridge at **Maentwrog**, a pleasant little village that takes its name from a prehistoric stone in the churchyard — *Maen* (stone) of Twrog. Now isolated from the sea, the village was once a busy little port for the slate from the surrounding hills.

Across the valley is Plas Tan-y-Bwlch, the Snowdonia National Park Study Centre. Set in beautiful woodlands, the house once belonged to the wealthy Oakley family, owners of the quarries of Blaenau Ffestiniog. The centre runs many courses open to the public on all aspects of the countryside and the National Park. A

Portmeirion

nature trail starts from the car park by the house and wanders up through the woods to Llyn Mair, a small reservoir above, returning eastwards close to the railway and back to the garden. A second trail starts at the lake and circles through the woodland for about three-quarters of a mile.

The lake, Llyn Mair (Mary's Lake), is an idyllic spot and can easily be approached by the steep road (B4410), past the Oakley Arms Hotel; there is a picnic area and car park and the rhododendrons are magnificent when in bloom. Just above is one of the stations for the Festiniog Railway which curves and winds its way through the woods of Tan-y-Bwlch.

The river meanders slowly down to **Penrhyndeudraeth** where it is crossed by a toll bridge and then out to sea by **Portmeirion**. This small private village with its tiny harbour was designed and built by the late Sir Clough Williams-Ellis, the Welsh architect whose intention was to create a place free from careless building and advertising. The cottages, mainly in the Italian style, are grouped around a small bay and contain many features collected from other

PLACES TO VISIT IN
THE VALE OF FFESTINIOG

PlasTan-y-Bwlch
Maentwrog, on A487
Snowdonia National Park Study
Centre, runs courses for visitors
on countryside and aspects of
the national park.
Nature trail to Llyn Mair.

Portmeirion
Off the A487 at Minffordd.
Beautiful Italianate village
conceived by Sir Clough
Williams-Ellis. Gardens, café
and craft shops. Where *The
Prisoner* was filmed.

buildings and saved for posterity. The hotel, the centrepiece of the
village, was sadly destroyed by fire in 1981, and, with it, many of Sir
Clough's drawings and records. The village has craft shops and
restaurants, and many of the cottages are available to rent. During
the 1960s the cult TV series *The Prisoner* was filmed here and there
is a small display of memorabilia in one of the cottages. It is on a
private estate but visitors are welcome, though charged; access is
off the A487 at Minffordd.

Across the sandy estuary from Portmeirion the hills rise steeply
to the lofty summits of the Rhinog range. It is a rugged range of hills
stretching twenty miles to the south, dotted here and there with little
lakes and woodlands, penetrated, but never crossed, by single-
track mountain roads. It follows the magnificent sweep of Cardigan
Bay right down to Barmouth (Abermaw).

At the northern end of the range the coastal land of Morfa
Harlech is wide, backed by huge sand dunes from which the sea
has retreated. The town of **Harlech** stands pinched between the

sea and the hills with the castle perched high on a rocky outcrop
dominating the surrounding area.

Built by Edward I in 1238 on the very edge of the bay the castle
must have served as a strong reminder to the Welsh of the power
of the king, for it is visible for many miles around. The sea has now
retreated, but it is nevertheless striking. It came under attack many
times from the Welsh before being taken in 1404 by Owain Glyndwr.
It served for some time as his capital before being re-taken by the

PLACES OF INTEREST
IN AND NEAR HARLECH

Harlech Castle
Fine castle in superb situation.
Scene of many bloody battles
and inspiration for the march
Men of Harlech.

**Muriaur Gwyddelod, Irish-
man's Walls**
Situated in fields south of
Harlech.
Remains of early Iron Age
settlements possibly Irish.

Llanfair Slate Caverns
2 miles south of Harlech on
A496.
Walk-in caverns of old slate
mine and see the real conditions.

Beaches
The whole of the bay in front of
Harlech has beautiful golden
sands with lots of room for
everyone.

English in 1408. During the Wars of the Roses the Lancastrians
held out there for eight years before fleeing overseas. One survivor,
a twelve-year-old boy, went on to become Henry VII, and it is said
that this siege inspired the march *Men of Harlech*. It was the last
Welsh fortress to be captured during the Civil War, but since then
has been left to become a ruin, a grand ruin however, with an inner
courtyard surrounded by two mighty walls surmounted by narrow
walkways. There are magnificent views over the estuary, the
mountains to the north and the Lleyn Peninsula. The castle is
approached from the town side to gain a full appreciation of the
difficulties faced by an attacker.

A short distance to the south of the town in the fields above the
road is Muriaur Gwyddelod or Irishman's Walls, believed to have
been built by settlers from Ireland between 1,000 and 2,000 years
ago. The walls are a circular enclosure about 4ft high and subdi-
vided into 'rooms'; there are several similarly named sites in North
Wales, but we can only guess their true origin.

The beaches along the bay below Harlech are some of the
finest; they are backed by sand dunes and are wide enough for the
most energetic game of football. Stretching from Harlech Point in
the north almost to Barmouth in the south, they are safe for bathing

Harlech Castle with the mountains of Snowdonia in the distance

PLACES OF INTEREST AROUND LLANBEDR

Llandanwg Church
Signposted from A496.
Ancient church on beach nearly buried by sand dunes.

Shell Island
Turn off A496 in Llanbedr opposite the youth hostel. Connected by causeway covered at high tide. Sand dunes and excellent beach with café and bars. Millions of shells to collect.

Roman Steps
Turn off at Victoria Hotel in Llanbedr.
At head of Cwm Bychan, footpath leads from lake to the steps. Remains of ancient packhorse trail with well preserved steps. Picnic spot at lakeside.

Maes Artro
Adjacent to A496 just south of Llanbedr.
Village containing workshops of craftsmen including weavers, potters, clockmakers and gold and silversmiths plus many more. You can watch them at work and buy if you wish. Aquaria, playgrounds and cafés, something for everyone.

and never crowded. Access to the beaches is from the A496 and is signposted. The Royal St David's golf course lies behind the dunes.

South of Harlech at **Llandanwg** (there is a car park right behind the dunes), an interesting medieval church lies buried by sand nearby. At **Llanbedr** the road to Shell Island is directly opposite the youth hostel and goes across a causeway which is covered at high tide. There is a charge to reach the island for day visitors, but, as may be guessed, it is a great spot to collect shells and enjoy the sea, and is ideal for children. Also in Llanbedr is Maes Artro, a commune of craftsmen and artists making everything from candles to gems. It is an imaginative scheme giving an opportunity to visitors to see many local craftsmen at work. There is a playground for children, an aquarium with specimens of locally found fish, and a restaurant, all pleasantly laid out in a small area of woodland.

It is thought that in prehistoric times this particular section of the coastline was the main landing spot for trade with Ireland. There are

The church at Llandanwg, almost buried in the sand dunes

Part of a Welsh village in traditional style, at the Maes Artro craft centre

many old tracks and roadways leading into and across the hills from Llandanwg and Llanbedr. Several tracks can be traced continuously into England. Many of the old tracks, now metalled roads into the hills, are steep and narrow but lead to some fascinating places.

One such road leaving Llanbedr beside the Victoria Hotel divides after a mile and a half. The right fork goes up to Cwm Nantcol, a beautiful isolated valley below Rhinog Fach and Rhinog Fawr and a good spot from which to ascend these mountains. The left fork follows the narrow wooded valley of the Afon Arto to the head of Cwm Bychan, where there is a parking spot by the lake; from here the famous Roman Steps can be followed. The footpath leads across the stream and through the woods to the start of the steps which lead over the shoulder of Rhinog Fawr before descending to the valley beyond. The steps are an interesting walk, particularly if at the highest point you turn left and walk into the hills to the north; the rock scenery is superb, with hugh perched rocks (glacial erratics) sometimes the size of small houses deposited on the glacier-polished granite. The steps are man-made, but there is no evidence that they are Roman. It is more likely that they were a medieval packhorse trail, though the route could very easily be the same as an earlier prehistoric track which can be traced and followed right through the hills to Bala.

Perhaps the finest road into the hills leaves the coast road from the village of **Llanfair**. It climbs easily for a mile or two, with several large standing stones beside the road, to the highest point with magnificent views over Harlech, the estuary and the Lleyn Peninsula beyond. The metalled road then dips down to the left around the hillside but directly in front is a rocky track, leading first to an Iron Age hillfort that crowns the hill Moel Geodog, and then continuing north into and across this range of mountains. There is a possibility that at one time this track was the main road to England from the coast and Ireland, for, though overgrown now, it is terraced into the hillside and paved across the marshes. There are many hut circles and standing stones along the route indicating its importance. If time allows, it makes a good (fairly easy) walk.

The metalled road, which can be followed more easily, runs at a high level parallel with the coast for about five miles to a small lake. From here a road to the left drops steeply down to rejoin the coast

'Roman Steps' at the head of Cwm Bychan

PLACES TO VISIT
AROUND BARMOUTH AND
THE MAWDDACH ESTUARY

RNLI Maritime Museum
On quay in Barmouth.
Lifeboat and other ship models,
old photographs.

Barmouth Estuary
Footpath across the railway
bridge over the estuary gives
good views of the estuary and
Cadair Idris to the south.

Old Country Life Centre
Off A496 at Tal-y-bont
Glimpses of bygone days in the
country with traditional tools,
crafts, fashions and other
aspects. Old mill now houses
restaurant and gift shop.

Weaver's Loft
Jubilee Road, Barmouth
Weaving shop producing
tapestries and tweed.

**Coed-y-Brenin Forest and
Visitor Centre**
Off A470 at Pont Dolgefeiliau.
Displays of forest fauna and
flora, and gold mining machinery. Plus many tracks of interest
in the forest and environs.

**Rhaedr Mawddach and
Pistyll Cain**
In the forest to the east, follow
the footpath from the picnic spot
at Pont Dolgefeiliau. Map obtain-
able at visitor centre as above.

road; or it is possible to continue on this minor road for several more
miles and return by the same route. This is a splendid drive though
care must be taken as the road is single track with few passing
places; it can be joined at several points by climbing steeply from
the coast road.

South from Llanbedr the busy road follows the wide coastal plain
to **Dyffryn Ardudwy**; here again there are significant prehistoric
remains: signposted to the east is Dyffryn Cairn, which when new
was estimated to be 100ft long and 54ft broad. The visible remains
are those of the burial chambers. Joining the A496 just after the
village is a minor road to the east which leads to further burial
chambers and several old drovers' routes across the hills. There
are many fine old trackways crossing these hills; almost certainly
the road south around the estuary was hazardous and only since

the coming of tourism and the railways has access to the coast been opened up. Keen walkers with a map and compass can be guaranteed a splendid day out on these hills, simply by following any of these trackways. They can have the hills to themselves all day with some of the finest scenery in the whole of Wales.

The main seaside resort along this coast is **Barmouth, (Abermaw)** squeezed tightly between the hills and the sea. It owes much of its popularity to the railway and the Victorian penchant for sea bathing, much of the architecture reflecting that era. The railway still plays an important part in the life of Barmouth, approaching the town from the south by an 800yd-long bridge across the estuary. There was a danger that the bridge, which is built on wooden piers, would have to be closed, as it was badly damaged by seaborne rot. Fortunately this has been arrested and for the time being the line has been saved. It has also been passed as fit to take occasional steam trains, which makes a magnificent sight as they cross in this fine setting. The bridge can be used by pedestrians for a small toll and is a recommended way to see the superb views around the estuary.

Today Barmouth is still a popular town in a beautiful setting; it has some fine beaches and whether approached by sea, road or rail, the scenery is breathtaking. The estuary of the Afon Mawddach is similar to a Norwegian fjord with its steeply wooded slopes and surrounding mountains. The road (A496) from Dolgellau, clinging in many places to the very edges of the shore, is particularly scenic with views across to Cadair Idris high above the opposite bank.

A few years ago a large multi-national mining company proposed to dredge the sand and silt of the estuary to extract the particles of gold that had been washed down from the surrounding hills. Although extensive tests and trials showed that gold did exist, its price at that time made the project unviable, and fortunately the idea was abandoned.

At the head of the estuary is the very Welsh market town of Dolgellau, a compact little town with narrow streets that seems to be the dividing line between North and Mid-Wales. Despite its position and its sixteenth-century bridge, it has figured little in Welsh history. The views to the south are commanded by the mighty summit of Cadair Idris (2,927ft). It is a good centre for exploring the

The hills on the northern side of the Mawddach Estuary have a number of abandoned gold mines

The neighbouring waterfalls of Pistyll Cain (right) and Rhaeadr Mawddach (below) with its small reservoir once used for the nearby gold workings

surrounding hills and valleys with a number of easy walks in the locality, details of which are available from the Tourist Information Centre.

Dolgellau will be described in detail in the next chapter. Meanwhile, retrace your steps slightly to the small village of **Llanelltyd** to the north-west. Now merely a junction of two major roads it was once the major crossing point of the Mawddach and it was perhaps

for this reason that in 1199 a Cistercian abbey was founded on the eastern bank. Little remains of Cymmer Abbey nowadays — a few walls and some of the thirteenth-century church — but it must have been a magnificent setting in its early years.

North from the abbey the steep-sided valley of the Mawddach is followed on the west by the A470 and on the east by a minor road. Both have their merits as they wind up the wooded valley following this renowned trout river. The 'A' road first reaches the highly recommended Tyn-y-Groes Hotel, well known to anglers, while the

minor road can be followed into the hills and forests (though a map should be taken to avoid getting lost), where there are some wonderful panoramas. The A470 can be rejoined at **Ganllwyd**.

This small hamlet is in the heart of the Coed-y-Brenin Forest, the Forest of Kings, the oldest and most extensive forest in North Wales. It is also in the heart of the gold prospecting area and though little is found nowadays, at one time the hills and valleys around were akin to the Klondyke.

The best place to learn more of both is to visit the Forestry Commission's Maesgwm Visitor Centre north of Ganllwyd, signposted off the road at the ancient bridge of Pont Dolgefeiliau. It is

L
$^1/_2$-2h
Forest
map
†††

most interesting, explaining the forest, the wildlife, and for those interested in the history of the area, the goldmining. The displays are well done and explanatory. There is also a splendid display of equipment used in the refining of gold. While there do pick up a leaflet on the forest walks and spend some time exploring. There are marked tracks and picnic sites, many just off the main road. It is a lovely area to visit, but allow plenty of time as there is much to enjoy in the forest.

The map available details over fifty miles of roadways and footpaths, but thoroughly recommended is the walk from the car

park by the bridge to the twin waterfalls of Pistyll Cain and Rhaeadr

Cymmer Abbey, Llanelltyd

Mawddach. These are not accessible by road but are well worth the effort. Between the two falls is the site of the gold smelting works and above the Mawddach (about half a mile) is an occasionally-worked gold mine. It is really a splendid area to explore. There are 16,000 acres of forest, mainly firs and spruces but much of the original woodland of old Welsh oaks is intermingled with the new. It is a place of peace, good walking and not too many people.

The road (A470) continues north through the forest and on to the high moorlands, a straight and easy drive allowing plenty of time to enjoy the views before reaching the village of **Trawsfynydd**. The village has achieved dubious fame by being the site of Britain's first inland nuclear power station. Standing on the shores of the nearby lake, the large square structure seems to fit well into the scenery, in many ways enhancing the nearby hills.

A short distance beyond the power station a small road goes off to the right under a railway bridge and between steep banks to a wood. Here by a gate are the mounds of a small Roman amphi-theatre, unique in Wales. It was part of the camp of Tomen-y-Mur, visible as a small mound across the field. It must have been an isolated posting for a legionary born and bred on the Mediterranean coast, especially when the north westerlies blew in the winter. Nevertheless it was in a fine position and perhaps he could take comfort from the beauty of the surrounding hills.

The main road now drops sharply back into the Vale of Ffestiniog, or turns right through Ffestiniog and Blaenau Ffestiniog to cross the Crimea Pass. The descent into the Lledr Valley is steep, but gives some splendid views of the southern slopes of Moel Siabod. Pass through Roman Bridge, which has no Roman connections, to **Dolwyddelan** and its small castle. Built about 1170 as the home of Llewelyn the Great, the castle has several interesting features, but is small compared with Edward's fortresses on the coast.

The road winds through the Gwydyr Forest to meet and cross the Afon Conwy close to Betws-y-Coed. A short distance upstream from the bridge is the Fairy Glen and Conwy Falls, easily approached by a pleasant path along the river bank. Above the falls, the river divides into the Afon Machno which turns south-west along the lovely Cwm Penmachno. The Afon Conwy continues up the valley for several more miles before turning south-west near Pentrefoelas.

L
1h
*
†††

Leaving the busy main road (A5) the Conwy turns towards its source, followed closely by a minor road. Halfway up the valley is the community of **Yspytty Ifan**. It was a hospice run by the Knights of St John for the pilgrims on their way to Bardsey Island, but there are now few traces of its past. Four miles to the south is Llyn Conwy, source of this famous river. The surrounding moorland was until the Dissolution a sanctuary and, despite the many passing pilgrims, was known for its lawlessness. Today the area is equally notorious; known as the Migneint it is a marshy plateau with few tracks, crossed only by the roads from Yspytty Ifan and Penmachno. Close to the junction is an old decorated well which has associations with the pilgrims.

To the south stand the two peaks of Arenig Fawr and Arenig Fach. The taller, Arenig Fawr, stands to the south of its smaller sister, separated by a road, stream and railway. The now disused railway was the main line from Ffestiniog to Bala and then into England. Running high above Cym Prysor from Trawsfynydd and

Memorial stone to the drowned Quaker village at Llyn Celyn

crossing a high viaduct which now seems quite out of place in these wild moorlands, it was a magnificent journey under full steam. The Afon Tryweryn runs towards Bala but was dammed early in the 1960s to form Llyn Celyn which now supplies water to Liverpool. Beneath the waters of the lake was the small community of Capel Celyn, a mainly Quaker village, from where many families left to settle in America with the Pilgrim Fathers. A small chapel and carved rock on the northern shore commemorate the village. Below the dam the river is used for international canoe races, the water level being controlled from the reservoir; it joins the Afon Dee at Bala.

The town of **Bala** was famous before the Industrial Revolution for its woollen stockings. It takes its name from the Welsh *bala* meaning outlet, for there the Dee starts its journey to the sea from the nearby lake. Despite its central position in Wales, at the junction of many old roads, Edward I seems to have found it strategically unimportant. There is a small mound or motte in the town believed

Statue of the Reverend Thomas Charles, founder of the British and Foreign Bible Society, in the main street, Bala

to be of Norman origin though there are doubts even about that.

It is a grey stone town with a wide main street and was for many years the home of the Reverend Thomas Charles (1755-1814), founder of the British and Foreign Bible Society and a pioneer of Methodism in North Wales; his statue stands in the main street. It continued as a Methodist stronghold when the Reverend Lewis Edwards started an academy in 1837 on the outskirts of the town for young Methodist ministers. Many other Methodists left the town to start a colony in Patagonia in 1865, founding the town of Trelew where the families still live and farm, using Welsh as their first language.

Modern Bala is something of a holiday centre, reflecting little of its Methodist upbringing. It stands at the head of Llyn Tegid or Bala Lake, the largest natural lake in Wales, a favourite spot for yachtsmen as the occasional strong south-westerly wind can give exhilarating sailing. Known also for the fishing, both fly and coarse, the lake yields a unique species called the gwyniad believed to be a survivor from the Ice Age. It is a small fish resembling a herring that spurns the rod and is only occasionally caught by net. There are several specimens in the White Lion Hotel in the town.

The roads on each side of the lake make this shoreline accessible for most of its length, with several pleasant picnic and parking areas off the minor road to the south. A comparatively recent addition along the southern bank is the Bala Lake Railway, a narrow gauge railway following the old main line which has steam and diesel engines running the full length of the lake. The main station is at **Llanuwchllyn** at the south end of the lake. The locomotives once worked the old North Wales slate quarries and ensconced in an open or closed carriage one can enjoy the magnificent mountain and lakeside scenery.

On the northern side of Llyn Tegid the main road A494 speeds between Bala and Barmouth, but for those with more time several metalled tracks across the hills towards Trawsfynydd provide an interesting and adventurous trip. Starting from Llanuwchllyn the recommended route follows the course of the Afon Lliw over to Bronaber and Trawsfynydd. Two miles up the left-hand side above the road is Castell Carndochan, possibly a Norman motte, but more likely the home of an unknown brigand. Nearby are the characteristic white spoil heaps from a nineteenth-century gold mine. The road climbs steeply into the very heart of the mountains following the course of an ancient highway before descending through the forests to Bronaber on the Trawsfynydd to Dolgellau road.

It is a wild mountain road passing through some beautiful countryside and forests. Walkers should be armed with the necessary Ordnance Survey maps, either sheet 124 or 125, and a compass. There are few tracks and fewer walkers, and one must be prepared. Please remember also that, though all the hills and countryside are within the Snowdonia National Park, most of the land is privately owned. Walls and fences should not be damaged.

H
all
day
***
†††

Lake Bala (Llyn Tegid)

8

SOUTHERN SNOWDONIA

M any visitors to the Snowdonia National Park tend to regard the northern mountains as the only area within the park boundaries. It does in fact stretch quite extensively down to the south of Dolgellau and Bala, taking in the superb ranges of hills of the Arans and Cadair Idris, the beautiful estuary of the Afon Dyfi and the steep coastline north of Tywyn to the Afon Mawddach.

Apart from the coastline with its beaches and resorts, which are always busy in the holiday season, the mountains and the whole inland area tends to be less frequented and less popular than northern Snowdonia. Visitors who do tour the area will be well rewarded. It is a compact area with steep hills and deep tranquil valleys. The towns and villages are small and typically Welsh; the mountains, which seem to dominate every view, have been described as some of the most beautiful in the country. Certainly this description would fit the Arans, which loom high above the southern end of Bala Lake. The visitor who likes to get a little off the beaten track will have ample opportunity; there are many fine mountain roads that cross high cwms and visit out-of-the-way lakes and valleys. There are nature reserves, quiet rivers and mountain walks. Once into the area the hills are all around, seemingly rolling on forever.

At the northern end of the area is Bala Lake and the small town

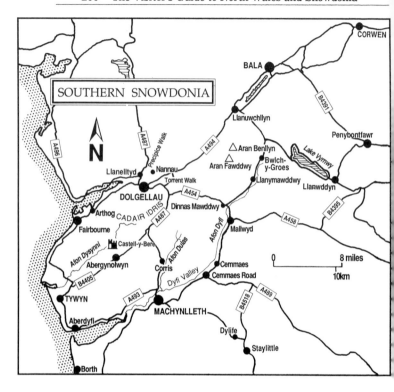

of Bala (see chapter 7, pages 195-7), which stands at the outflow of the lake into the Afon Dee. The lake, also called Llyn Tegid, is roughly four miles long by half a mile wide and lies pleasantly though undramatically below rolling green hills with the ever present Arans commanding the southern view.

The A494 trunk road to Dolgellau follows the northern shoreline before ascending two miles south of the lake to the old farmhouse of Pont Gwyn right on the watershed. It is said that a raindrop on one side of the roof runs to the Dee and the Irish Sea and one on the other flows south to join the Afon Wnion and thence to the Maw and Cardigan Bay. The Wnion flows down a beautiful narrow wooded valley, a land of forest-clad hills and rocky precipices. The road hugs the steep side of the river and the now defunct railway (closed in 1965) fights for space between road and river. It is a lovely journey — British Rail must be sadly regretting closing some of their more picturesque lines. Towards Dolgellau the valley widens marginally and Cadair Idris comes into view over the hilltops, its rampart-like ridges giving it an appearance of strength towering above the valley. After twenty miles the river descends to the flood plain and finally joins the broad estuary of the Afon Mawddach and so to the sea. It has been a tossing, tumbling journey through some of the finest scenery in Wales.

An alternative road leaves Bala's main street and crosses the northern shores of the lake, ideal for photographers, and then traverses round the quieter southern lakeside to Llanuwchllyn, home of the Bala Lake Railway which, utilising the old trackway, has regular trips along the lakeside.

A single track road leaves Llanuwchllyn heading almost due south. Signposted Dinas Mawddwy it climbs gradually past the lower slopes of the Arans up the beautiful Cwm Cynllwyd to the summit of the pass. This is the infamous Bwlch-y-Groes, the highest road in Wales at 1,790ft. At the summit is a rather dismal parking area close to the peat hags. It is a bleak spot on a cold day, further spoilt by the signs refusing access to the nearby mountains. To the west can be seen the craggy ridge of the Arans. In times gone by the moorlands were famous for the peat gathered for fuel. Apparently some of the best in the land, it was hauled downhill by pony and sledge.

In 1850, when George Borrow was taking his leave of his host in Bala to traverse this same route, he was warned that his journey that day 'would be very rough over hills and mountains which constituted upon the whole the wildest part of all Wales'. This is still true today — the journey, though more comfortable, is just as awe inspiring in these superb hills.

The Arans, two magnificent peaks, rise sheer to the west, almost twins in shape and height. Formed of a volcanic ridge which runs between Dinas Mawddwy and Bala Lake they are the focus of one of the finest mountain walks south of the Snowdon massif. Aran Benllyn, the northernmost at 2,970ft and Aran Fawddwy, slightly less at 2,901ft, are best done as a complete traverse to appreciate

The notorious Bwlch-y-Groes descending to Pennant

H
5-6h
****
††††

their finer qualities. It is easier to start from the northern end close to Llanuwchllyn, where the gradual climb opens expanding vistas with each step. The summit views are unrivalled in Wales: the Berwyns to the east and Arenigs and even Snowdon to the north, Cadair Idris to the west and to the south a never ending view of rolling hills. The descent recommended would be to follow the ridge south to Cym Cywarch, though this does require extra transport; alternatively, return north to where you started the walk.

Motorists journeying south from the Bwlch-y-Groes will find their trip equally enjoyable and exciting, though the descent is a trifle worrying for the nervous. Close to the summit is a small, single track road signposted Lake Vyrnwy leading off to the east. This is a fine mountain road that gently follows a small stream. There is limited parking but some fine picnic spots in lovely settings. Eventually the bumpy road descends to the lake.

The lake is in fact a reservoir, opened in 1888 to supply water to Liverpool. It was formed by building a massive dam on a natural ridge across the end of the valley. The old village in the valley,

The dam and overflow at Lake Vyrnwy

PLACES TO VISIT IN SOUTHERN SNOWDONIA

The Arans
Two magnificent peaks between Dinas Mawddwy and Bala Lake which provide one of the finest mountain walks south of Snowdon.

Bwlch-y-Groes
The summit of the highest road in Wales at 1,790ft. Bleak on a cold day, and no access from here to the nearby mountains, but the climb up Cwm Cynllwyd to the summit is beautiful.

Llyn Vyrnwy
Reservoir in a beautiful setting. Largest nature reserve in Wales, administered by the RSPB, with visitor centre, marked trails and picnic spots.

Ffrwd Fawr Waterfall
Near Dylife
The most spectacular fall in Wales, but difficult to get a good view, and the descent to the base on foot is hazardous.

Pistyll Gwyn
A fine waterfall a mile to the west of Llanymawddwy along a pleasant track.

Merion Woollen Mill
Dinas Mawddwy
Huge craft shop and display of weaving traditional tapestries.

Plas Machynlleth
Machynlleth
House originally built in 1653 in fine grounds. Houses local government offices and exhibition of Welsh crafts.

Centre for Alternative Technology
Machynlleth
Fascinating centre demonstrating the possibilities of living on a small share of the earth's resources. Much of interest, bookshop and restaurant.

Corris Railway Museum
Corris
Collection of memorabilia and

Llanwddyn, was first rebuilt below the dam, then the earlier houses and church were demolished and the villagers evacuated to the new village. Nowadays it is a beautiful setting — the lake formed is roughly four miles long, contains 12,000 million gallons of water and covers 1,100 acres. The area surrounding the lake is a nature reserve, the largest in Wales, and is administered by the Royal

material relating to the slate
quarries and their railways.

Foel Friog Picnic Site
Aberllefeni
An idyllic and peaceful spot,
ideal for children. Several
waymarked tracks into the Dyfi
Forest nearby.

Tal-y-Llyn Railway
One of the 'Great Little Trains of
Wales'. Travels inland for seven
miles, skirting the hills and valley
of the Afon Fathew.

Castell-y-Bere
Dysynni Valley
Stands on large promontory
rock near the head of the valley.
Begun in 1221 but eventually
captured by Edward I and
destroyed in 1294. Fine ruins,
with original layout still evident.

Fairbourne and Barmouth
Steam Railway
Rebuilt engines from all over the
world. Regular service along the
coast to the Mawddach Estuary
in summer.

Butterfly Safari
Fairbourne Station
Collection of free-flying butter-
flies from Africa, America and
Asia. Also small mammals.

Creggennen
Twin lakes at about 800ft, in a
shallow depression below
Cadair Idris. Small car park and
free access to banks of lake.

Precipice Walk, New Precipice
Walk and Torrent Walk
Near Dolgellau
Three fine walks with magnifi-
cent views.

Penmaenpool Wildlife Centre
Near Dolgellau
In former railway signal box
alongside Mawddach estuary,
run by RSPB and North Wales
Wildlife Trust. Information centre
and observation point.
Also Morfa Mawddach Railway
Walk along disused railway line
on the south side of the estuary.

Society for the Protection of Birds who have converted an old
Calvinistic chapel close to the dam into a visitor centre. There are
many marked trails and maps are available of recommended
routes.

L
1-2h
*
†††

A narrow road circumnavigates the lake with several picnic
spots. Visitors are encouraged, though as the water is for drinking

Bunant Fawr, a beautiful spot on the moors above Lake Vyrnwy

The Vale of Dyfi north of Machynlleth

they must beware of causing any form of pollution, so boating and swimming are forbidden. From most viewpoints the Gothic-style draw-off tower gives an almost fairly tale impression to the surroundings. Many of the hillsides have been planted with mixed woodlands, further enhancing the scene and creating natural cover for wildlife and birds.

The lake can also be approached from the village of **Penybontfawr** in the Tanat Valley. It must be said that no matter what approach is taken, the roads are narrow and care must be exercised.

Returning to the Bwlch-y-Groes, the descent south into the valley is not for the faint hearted. The road is in a superb situation, terraced down the hillside. The hills, craggy and rough with deeply incised streams, give an air of grandeur to this fine cwm. It is a steep and narrow road with few passing places so care must be taken.

M
$\frac{1}{2}$-1h
**
††††

Shortly before the valley bottom is reached there is a sharp bend in the road. If you can park here or close by, a small path leads uphill following a fence to Llaethnant (Milk Valley) at the very head of the valley. Presumably the name relates to the beauty of the setting. The infant Dyfi flows from the high cwm below Aran Fawddwy over a series of small waterfalls and pools before starting its more leisurely flow to the sea. Some of the pools are ideal for paddling — the valley is sheltered and delightful on a warm sunny day.

Until very recently an enterprising local farmer had a small hydro-electric generator at the head of the valley providing electricity to the local farms and the nearby village of Llanymawddwy. He was the last private supplier in Wales; now it is operated by the local electricity board.

L
1-2h
**
†††

At last the road levels out and wanders easily along the valley bottom, first through **Llanymawddwy**, a hamlet on the Afon Dyfi. Close to the village are some fine waterfalls, notably Pistyll Gwyn, a mile to the west along a pleasant little track which starts by the church. The river is often known as the Royal Dyfi but whether it is because of the magnificent setting or the trout fishing is open to speculation; it is certainly a king of rivers.

There are many tempting places to stop along this tranquil valley before reaching **Dinas Mawddwy**. This small town, which had a fearsome reputation, lies in a lovely amphitheatre below wooded

The Merion Mill, Dinas Mawddwy

hills; during the flowering season much of the hillside is coloured by a breathtaking display of rhododendrons. The quiet little town, no longer fortified as its name would indicate, huddles along a wide main street and was once the centre for the nearby lead mining industry. In the sixteenth century the area was notorious for the red-haired thieves of Mawddwy who terrorised North Wales in the sixteenth century, plundering, pillaging and killing throughout the land until eventually they were caught in 1555 when eighty of the bandits were condemned to death.

Their reputation still lingers however, and amongst this wild scenery it is easy to conjure up the past. The local pub, The Red Lion, has a Brass Room full of old horse brasses and other collectable brass items. It is also known locally for its excellent restaurant.

Close to the Dyfi bridge just below the village is the terminus of the railway which closed in 1950. The old engine sheds now house a woollen mill open to the public with a huge craft shop and a display of weaving traditional tapestries; the station building is a café.

Mallwyd church with a whale rib hanging above the porch

The imposing clock tower at the end of the main street in Machynlleth

To the west of Dinas Mawddwy the busy A470 trunk road climbs up and over the Bwlch Oerddrws, with fine views of the southern hills and Cadair Idris before descending to the old coaching inn of Cross Foxes and then down to Dollgellau. It provides one of the main access roads into Wales from Shrewsbury and is a lovely journey through some of the best Welsh scenery.

Mallwyd just to the south of Dinas Mawddwy has a Brigands Inn, named to commemorate the Red Robbers. The church, close to the pub, has a whale's rib hanging in the porch (which is dated

1641), dug up locally in the nineteenth century. Its early history is vague, but how it came to be in the area is open to speculation.

Still following the Afon Dyfi the valley begins to open out and the hills become less dominant, the road winding easily now through the small villages of Cemmaes and Cemmaes Road before arriving at Machynlleth. To the north of this route is the huge expanse of the Dyfi Forest, which seems to cloak the upper slopes and even the summits of the hills.

Machynlleth, pronounced Ma'hun'hleth, is a smallish market town serving a very widespread population. It has an open atmosphere and a wide main street, at the end of which stands a large decorative clock tower. Built in 1872 to commemorate the coming of age of Lord Londonderry's heir, it is an elaborate structure which would no doubt cause the planning authorities a headache in this present age. The Londonderrys lived in a large house, Plas Machynlleth, just off the main street, which has been developed since its original foundation in 1653. It stands in fine grounds and was latterly donated to the town by the family, now housing local government offices and an exhibition of Welsh crafts. The gardens consist of a pleasant park open to the public.

Across the main street is the Owain Glyndwr Institute, a Tourist Information Centre and library, and adjacent is an older building known as Parliament House which is reputed to be the place where Owain Glyndwr held his first parliament in 1404. It was at this gathering that he first laid down his plans for an independent Wales with its own laws and universities. Sadly for him he never saw his dream come to fruition, though many Welsh people would still seek to achieve his goals.

A small mountain road signposted Dylife leaves the eastern end of the main street to follow an ancient trackway the route of which has changed little. It crosses a golf course to Forge before following the narrow valley of the Afon Dulas and climbing steeply to pick its way along a series of ridges giving splendid views of the rolling hills all around. To the south is Plynlimon, source of many rivers including the Severn. There is evidence of prehistoric man at the high point of the road, and just above is Bryn-y-Fedwen with some ancient burial mounds.

From the summit the road descends to the now almost deserted village of **Dylife**, once a bustling township in the eighteenth and nineteenth centuries when over 1,000 people lived here, mining the lead and sending it by horse drawn wagon to Machynlleth. There were three or four inns, several chapels, a church and a school to provide for their needs; there is one pub, The Star Inn, and a few isolated houses left. During its working life the mine is said to have had some of the best working conditions in the country, but now only a rather ugly site remains.

Below Dylife and just by the road is the Ffrwd Fawr waterfall. It is difficult to get a good view and the descent on foot to the base is hazardous but it certainly is the most spectacular fall in Wales. The difficulty of access has ensured that it remains relatively undisturbed. The water drops clear into a deeply incised rocky canyon before pouring over a series of cataracts to the gentler valley below. There is a small viewing platform close to the road but do take care.

Above Dylife is a small Roman fortlet which sits atop a rounded hill, again an indication of the antiquity of this roadway and its importance in the past. Penycroben hilltop is accessible by a footpath that starts close to the road junction in the village, a right turn along the ridge brings you to the summit and the Roman camp. Little remains to be seen; the walls of the fort were originally turf banks. During excavations in 1960 Roman pots were found, but no evidence to prove that they were aware of the lead ore to be found M locally. The name means Gibbet Hill, as later it was used for public 1h executions until the early nineteenth century. The trackway crosses ** the summit before a right turn returns you to the village. ††††

There are many small mountain roads in this area for those who prefer to get off the beaten track and explore a little but it is also worth returning to Machynlleth and heading north to the Dyfi Bridge, built originally in 1533 but later strengthened, to the road junction. The road to the west follows the Dyfi downstream to Aberdyfi and its estuary. For the moment however, take the northern route up through the valley of another Afon Dulas. This, like most of the roads hereabouts, winds up a narrow wooded valley with steep-sided hills on each side. A minor road runs parallel along the opposite side of the river and gives access to perhaps the most unusual visitor centre in Snowdonia.

Tucked away in a magnificent old slate quarry is the Centre for

A demonstration of solar panels at the Centre for Alternative Technology

❄ Alternative Technology. It is a demonstration centre showing the possibilities of living on only a small share of the earths resources with a minimum of pollution and waste. It creates its own energy with windmills and solar panels, it grows much of its own food organically and shows the possibilities of re-cycling much of the waste we create in everyday living. It demonstrates a more economical way of life both in monetary cost and the saving of the earth's resources. It is altogether a fascinating place with much to offer the visitor in its displays and mode of life. There is a restaurant and bookshop with free parking; allow plenty of time for your visit — you will be truly surprised by the alternatives offered to 'normal' lifestyles.

🚶 L

1h
*
††

If you can tear yourself away, the Dulas valley still has much in store. There is a pleasant little picnic site at **Tan-y-Coed** which is the start of a waymarked walk which can be extended to the high moorlands ridge beyond. **Corris**, a small village standing at the confluence of the Dulas and a small tributary and dominated by tips from the surrounding slate workings, is the home of the Corris

Railway Museum. It houses a collection of rolling stock (especially

Corris and the surrounding Dyfi Forest

their almost unique slate waggons), memorabilia and material relating to the nearby slate quarries and their railways. A length of track has been reinstated.

L-M
¹/₂-2h
**
†††

A minor road follows the Afon Dulas north to **Aberllefeni** giving access to the Dyfi Forest. Just short of the village is the Foel Friog picnic site, ideal for children and an idyllic spot far from the madding crowd. Close by are several waymarked tracks into the forest. Guides to the walks and the forest can usually be bought at local shops — it is a vast area so do take care not to get lost.

Take the main road from Corris to come first to the junction with the Tal-y-Llyn valley at Minffordd and then climb steeply over the rugged shoulder of Cadair Idris to descend to Cross Foxes and so to Dolgellau.

The alternative route from Machynlleth and Dyfi Bridge follows the Afon Dyfi, first across the wide river valley and then tightly along the very side of the estuary sharing the narrow bank with the main line railway. The estuary to the south is an important site for the study of wildfowl and migrant waders; the marshes across the estuary are part of the Dyfi National Nature Reserve and contain much, beside wildfowl, of scientific interest. Most of the area has restricted access and is maintained by the Royal Society for the Protection of Birds.

Aberdyfi is a small coastal resort hugging the side of the estuary. It is a colourful little town huddled along the quayside. A venue for yachtsmen and holidaymakers it still manages to retain its very Welsh feel. The quay is a busy little place catering for the Outward Bound School of Wales who provide courses in sailing, canoeing and climbing locally. Close by is a wide sandy beach which stretches some way up the coast.

The town is immortalised in the song *The Bells of Aberdovey* from Charles Dibdins' opera *Liberty Hall*, based on an old Welsh legend that below the sea lies an old village and church, drowned many years ago, but the bells of the church still peal. The legend first appears in the thirteenth century, but became popular with writers in the romantic period of the eighteenth and nineteenth centuries.

The road and railway continue to follow the coast past the well known golf course to **Tywyn**, a rather bleak town that has become a popular seaside resort with a wide sand and shingle beach.

The Dolgoch viaduct of the Tal-y-Llyn Railway

Perhaps its main claim to fame is that it is the terminus for the Tal-y-Llyn Railway, one of the 'Great Little Trains of Wales'.

The railway opened in 1865 to serve the slate quarries in the Tal-y-Llyn valley. It starts at Tywyn Wharf station, where there is a museum with many exhibits from the heyday of narrow gauge railways. Saved from closure by volunteers the line travels inland, skirting the hills and valley of the Afon Fathew for just over seven miles. There are several stations en route and at **Dolgoch** the railway crosses an impressive viaduct to the station. A scenic walk to the Dolgoch waterfalls makes a pleasant excursion, with a not too steep climb up through the woods. The line continues to **Nant**

Aberdyfi and the estuary

L
½-2h
*

†††

Gwernol, where there are extensive forest walks above the terminus at **Abergynolwyn**.

The narrow valley can also be followed by car, though the journey may be more fraught for the road is narrow and busy in summer. The walks to the falls can easily be reached from the roadside, as can those in the forest above Abergynolwyn, from convenient car parks at both points. From the village a trackway can be followed to the south up to the old Bryneglwys slate quarry for which the railway was originally built.

Continuing up the valley will bring you to Tal-y-Llyn (lake), a pleasant spot with many places to picnic and relax along its shoreline. In fine weather the lake is ideal for swimming and there are two hotels close by. The steep southern slopes of Cadair Idris rise sharply from the lake to dominate the surrounding countryside. The finest ascent of this mountain starts in the valley just north of the lake close to Minffordd, which will be described later.

Parallel with the valley of the Tal-y-Llyn, accessible on the minor road north-west and signposted from Abergynolwyn, is the Dysynni

Tal-y-Llyn

Valley; more open and with wider views it has a charm of its own.
Dominated by the great mountain to the north it is peaceful and
more rural, in sharp contrast to its past when it was swept by the
great glaciers descending from the north.

In this isolated valley, now far from the mainstream of Welsh
political life, Llewelyn the Great built what was to be one of the most
important of Welsh castles, Castell-y-Bere. Carefully designed and
ornately constructed, it stands on a large promontory of rock near
the head of the valley. Begun in 1221, it saw many Welsh rulers,
some optimistic some despairing, before Edward I crushed so
many hopes in 1277. Dafydd, brother of Llewelyn and the last Welsh
prince, established himself at the castle and continued his forays
against the English. The enraged Edward sent his armies after
Dafydd and the castle became the last point of resistance for the
Welsh people. Eventually captured, the castle fell to Edward and
was finally destroyed in 1294, its short but turbulent history over.
The ruins are rather grand on their rocky crest, and the original
layout is still evident with three ruined towers and a rectangular

keep. It is difficult to imagine that this peaceful valley played such a significant part in Welsh history.

Looming large above the lower reaches of the valley is Craig-y-Aderyn, Bird Rock, a sharp crag that is a remnant from the days when this low lying valley was an arm of the sea. It is still a breeding place for cormorants and is protected by the RSPB.

A fine road, which in the South of France would be described as a corniche, follows the coastline north. High above the sea it hugs the steep hillside with some fine views across Cardigan Bay before reaching **Borth** and later **Fairbourne**, two coastal resorts that are more in the English style than Welsh. They are a collection of caravan sites and holiday bungalows that, though busy in summer, lie dormant for much of the year.

Fairbourne, like its close neighbour Tywyn, is the home of a narrow gauge railway. The Fairbourne and Barmouth Steam Railway is a major award winner and visitor attraction; it has has been reconstucted to a 12½in gauge and the trains are pulled by scale replicas of famous narrow gauge locomotives based on both British and foreign prototypes. During the summer a regular service operates along a two-mile stretch of the coast north to the Mawddach estuary, where an adjoining ferry will take you across the waters to Barmouth before returning. The stations on the line are re-created in Victorian style and much of the equipment is manufactured in the railway's own workshop.

A recent additional attraction at the station is the Butterfly Safari. Housed in a purpose-made building are free flying butterflies from Africa, America and Asia. An adjacent collection houses a range of small mammals such as racoons, lemurs and wildcats. Regardless of the weather, the atmosphere is carefully controlled and it can be an ideal family day out. Tickets are available at the station to cover both attractions.

A short distance to the north of Fairbourne, close to the wide marshlands of the estuary, is the small village of **Arthog**, its terraced houses hugging the roadside; a single track road climbs steeply from the village past Arthog Hall and waterfalls. Following the stream it rises quickly to reach the twin lakes of Cregennen at about 800ft. It is a lovely spot, the scenery so different from that of the coast a short distance away. It can also be much cooler. The

Eldon Square, Dolgellau

lakes and the countryside around them were given to the National Trust in 1959 by Major C.L. Wynne-Jones in memory of his two sons who had been killed in the war.

Cregennen sits in a shallow depression below the steep flanks of Cadair Idris; there is a small car park and free access to the banks of the lake. A large log cabin on the shore of the lake was imported from Canada in the late nineteenth century and erected here by the Wynne-Jones family. It can be booked for holidays from the National Trust.

An impressive looking hill, Bryn Brith (1,256ft) stands to the north of the lakes, which can be ascended easily by the wide footpath up the ridge. Cadair Idris, which dominates the whole scene, can be climbed from this side, though it must be quite a daunting ascent as the slope here is at its steepest.

M
1-1¹/₂h
*
†††

Past Cregennen the road wanders around the contour of Cadair giving some fine views of the mountain and also access to several footpaths which lead upwards towards its summit. Passing the small but pleasantly situated Gwernan Lake and hotel, it finally

Cadair Idris and the Cregennen lakes

descends easily to Dolgellau.

The main centre and market town for a much of the surrounding mountain district, **Dolgellau** can be very busy in summer. Several main roads meet here and at one time all used to pass through the centre of the town, but a bypass now alleviates at least some of this traffic. It is a very Welsh town, despite its popularity with visitors, clustered around its central square with its grey stone and slate buildings.

Despite being the major town in the old county of Merioneth and at the main crossing point of the Afon Wnion it seems to have figured little in Welsh history. In 1405 Owain Glyndwr is said to have held the last Welsh Parliament here, though the house in which it was reputed to have been held was dismantled in 1882 to make way for a shop and removed bodily to Newtown.

Within a short distance of the town are several shorter walks that have been popular since Victorian times. Perhaps the most famous is the Precipice Walk, a three-mile walk which circles Foel Cynwch just to the north of the river. The start is best made from near to the

Cadair Idris

M
1½-2h
*
††††

entrance of Nannau Park on the Dolgellau to Llanfachreth Road, where there is a car park and picnic spot. The route is clearly signposted and follows a terraced route around the hill. It is a delightful stroll, giving some of the best views across the Mawddach estuary and to Cadair Idris in the south. The walking is easy and though airy is safe for children. There are no major climbs involved and if care is taken the path is safe.

M
2-3h
*
†††

Another fine circular walk is the New Precipice Walk, which can be completed in about three hours. From **Llanelltyd** take a path to the right over a hump-backed bridge, bear left until you reach a lake, then head towards a house high on the mountainside. This path leads to a mountain road which drops down to the main road at Penmaenpool. This walk also has spectacular views.

L
1-2h
*
††

The Torrent Walk follows the deep glen of the Clydewog, starting at the junction with the Afon Wnion about one and a half miles east of Dolgellau. Approach down a minor road which leaves the A470 about a mile out of Dolgellau, or alternatively there is a small car park just after turning off to Brithdir, in which case the walk will be downstream. The well made path follows the narrow river as it tumbles down deep clefts and cataracts. It is a lovely walk at any time.

A couple of miles downstream from Dolgellau, where a toll road crosses the Afon Mawddach over a wooden bridge, is the Penmaenpool Wildlife Centre in a former railway signal box with an information centre and observation point. The wildlife centre is owned by the Snowdonia National Park, but is administered jointly by the Royal Society for the Protection of Birds and the North Wales Wildlife Trust, who provide telescopes and binoculars for public use.

When the railway line closed down in 1965 the NationalPark purchased the section from Dolgellau to Morfa Mawddach and converted it to a walk along the south side of the estuary. For those who like guided walks the RSPB lead groups along the Railway Walk during the summer, as well as walks through their bird reserve at Coed Garth Gell at the northern end of the Penmaenpool toll bridge.

Throughout this area Cadair Idris dominates the view. It is a huge mountain that seems to loom above the surrounding countryside no matter where you are. It is one of the great Welsh mountains

Penmaenpool toll bridge and former signal box

and though not quite as high as the earlier mentioned Arans it seems to have much more presence. After Snowdon it is perhaps the most climbed mountain in the National Park.

Cadair Idris, the 'Chair of Idris', is named, according to legend, after the giant Idris who was at once astronomer, poet and philosopher. His 'chair' is reputed to be the precipitous hollow between the summit and Llyn-y-Gadair, his observatory, a chamber formed by massive rocks. Whoever spends a night in his chair is said to awake as a poet or a madman.It can only be hoped that Idris is a friendly giant, as the mountain is very popular with walkers; its summit is marked by a huge cairn amongst a chaotic jumble of rocks and the views are superior to those of any mountain in Wales, those to the north being the best. On a clear day it is possible to see the Rhinogs range running south to north, and beyond them most of the mountains in the Snowdon massif. To the north-east are the Arenigs and the Arans and further east are the hills of Shropshire, the Long Mynd and the Wrekin; to the south are the Radnor forest and the mountains of central Wales. The whole of the coastline from

The sign which is to be seen at the boundaries of the Snowdonia National Park

the Lleyn Peninsula in the north to St Davids Head in the south should be visible on a clear day, and you may be very lucky and see across the sea to Ireland and the Wicklow Hills. It is certainly a magnificent prospect.

The ascent of this great hill can be made from most points of the compass. Some paths are famous, others less favoured, but all will bring you to the summit with a little effort. Go prepared on this mountain, as there is no railway or summit café to reward your efforts. The paths are reasonably well signposted where they leave the road and are quite well worn as they ascend; it is possible in some cases to reach the summit by one of them and descend by an alternative. Those contemplating climbing Cadair Idris should arm themselves with the Ordnance Survey Outdoor Leisure Map No 23 *Cadair Idris Area*, which is excellent and can only increase the enjoyment of their day. They should also allow for at least four hours walking to appreciate the mountain, and go prepared for cooler weather on the summit.

The mountain is in fact a long ridge, precipitous and craggy on its northern face, but more gently sloped to the south. The summit is Penygadair at 2,927ft. It stands on a narrow section of the ridge high above the cwm or seat of Idris. Llyn-y-Gadair lies to the north and the great bowl of Llyn Cau is to the south.

Two famous ascents start from the northern side of the mountain. In Victorian and Edwardian times the Foxes Path was popular, starting from Dolgellau and walking along the road, though nowadays most people would opt to park at Gwernan Lake and take the footpath opposite which climbs quite steeply to the Llyn-y-Gadair then more steeply up a jumble of boulders to reach the summit.

The Pony Path commences close to a car park at Ty-Nant about a mile south of Foxes Path. It climbs in a more leisurely way at first, but more steeply as it nears the ridge. Here it meets the path coming up from the south and turns east to climb steeply to the summit. The Foxes Path could be taken as an alternative means of descent.

The very fit might like to contemplate doing the whole ridge, starting at Cross Foxes Hotel in the north and heading south over all the summits to finish on the coast near Fairbourne. It would be a superb walk.

On the southern side of the mountain one of the more popular climbs is the Minffordd Path, beginning pleasantly in the valley just to the north of Tall-y-Llyn (lake). A path leaves the roadside close to Minffordd and climbs quite steeply up to Llyn Cau, a haunting spot, a dark lake set in a deep craggy cwm. You can rest awhile now, as the path follows the edge of the lake and is relatively flat before climbing very steeply out and onto the ridge below the summit. An easy but steep ascent leads to the cairn and refuge shelter. This is the best though steepest ascent, full of interest and with some fine situations.

Llanfihangel — a trackway — is the longest ascent, but also the least steep. Starting at the head of the valley north of Castell-y-Bere, it ascends easily alongside the Afon Cadair and along the flanks of the hills to meet the Pony Path on the summit ridge. Turning to the east it climbs to the summit. The early part of the trackway follows the line of the ancient packhorse trail which continued over the ridge to Dolgellau.

Many keen walkers will doubtless be able to find alternative routes to those suggested. Whichever way you decide to go, it is certain that you will have a memorable day with, weather permitting, one of the best views in the country as your reward.

The whole of the southern section of Snowdonia is in sharp contrast to the rest of North Wales. The scenery is superb, the villages are smaller and more homely and you must to a greater extent be prepared to explore to get the most from the countryside. There is something for everyone, and the effort required is always worthwhile. Every area has its own particular character, each slightly different from its neighbour, but all can be appreciated in their own right and in their own special way.

USEFUL INFORMATION
FOR VISITORS

ACCOMMODATION

There is a great range of accommodation available in North Wales, everything from caravans and guest houses to luxury hotels. Many visitors will have booked their stay in advance, but for those who cannot, or are content to tour without prior booking, many Tourist Information Centres offer a bed booking service. This service is designed to give information on type, style and prices of accommodation and recommends the most suitable for your requirements. If you prefer to scout about for your own accommodation the Tourist Information Centres can generally supply a list of hotels, guest houses and other beds available in the locality.

Youth Hostels

Throughout North Wales there is a chain of Youth Hostels. These are ideal for all ages, and are not restricted to young people. They are cheap to stay at and are generally in beautiful situations. The dormitory accommodation is excellent and meals can usually be provided.

There are hostels at:

Clwyd
Chester
Colwyn Bay
Corris
Cynwyd
Llangollen
Maeshafn

Gwynedd
Bala
Bangor
Betws-y-Coed
Bryn Gwynant, Beddgelert
Capel Curig
Ffestiniog
Harlech

Idwal Cottage
Kings, Dolgellau
Llanbedr
Llanberis
Lledr Valley, Dolwyddaelan
Penmaenmawr
Pen-y-Pass near Snowdon
Rowen
Snowdon Ranger

For further information and leaflets covering all aspects of youth hostelling in North Wales contact the regional office:
YHA Area Office
12 Wynnstay Road
Colwyn Bay
Clwyd
LL29 8NB
☎ (0492) 531406

ARCHAEOLOGICAL SITES

North Wales has many sites that may be of interest to visitors who are keen on history and prehistory. There are trackways, burial sites, hill forts and many standing stones and hut circles. Most are marked on Ordnance Survey maps and most are documented in separate guidebooks, which can only add to your tour of Wales and provide some good short walks and excursions. Here are a few of the major sites:

Clwyd

Elisegs Pillar
Llangollen
1,000-year-old carved pillar relating tale of early Welsh Prince Eliseg in field west of Valle Crucis Abbey.

Maen Achwyfan
Whitford
1 mile west of village
Eleventh-century wheel cross with fine carvings.

Offa's Dyke
Linear earthwork that runs parallel with English border. Bank and ditch now not too evident. Also a long-distance footpath.

Gwynedd

Capel Garmon
Neolithic burial chamber in fine situation on hills above and to east of Betws-y-Coed. Easily accessible on foot.

Harlech
The area behind Harlech, accessible by mountain road, has some fine hut circles and standing stones. There is also an Iron Age hillfort at Moel Coedog. South at Dyffryn Ardudwy are good examples of burial chambers.

Muriau'r Gwyddelod
Just off road south of Harlech. Huts, circles and enclosures possibly of early Irish settlers. Sometimes known as Irishman's Walls, they also occur in other locations.

Roman Steps
At Cwm Bychan, inland from Llanbedr, there is a line of steps going over the mountain pass. They are unlikely to be Roman, but are still very old.

Tomen-y-Mur
Near Trawsfynydd
Roman amphitheatre and encampment with later motte on same site.

Tre'r Ceiri
North of Nefyn on the Rivals (Yr Eifl). Superb remains of Iron Age fortified township with stone walls. Steep climb from road but worth it. Unprotected and now getting vandalised.

Anglesey
The island has a wealth of prehistory, evident particularly in the southern corner and on Holy Island.

Bryn-Celli-Ddu
Near Llanfair PG
Chamber and small mound now remaining of much larger construction.

Caer Gybi
Holyhead
Roman fort almost intact with high walls and towers. Later St Gybi's church built within walls.

Din Llugwy
Near Moelfre
Fortified village of variety of huts, well preserved in fine setting with other antiquities in vicinity.

Holyhead Mountain Hut Circles
Close to car park on South Stack road.
Some hut circles remaining of large farming village occupied from neolithic to Roman times.

BUS SERVICES

Sherpa Service
A regular bus service operating around Snowdon during summer for walkers and visitors. Runs from Caernarfon, Llanrwst or Porthmadog from May-September. Timetable from Tourist Office or Bus Station.

At least twenty different bus companies operate within the regions. Many have a smart new livery of red at the front and bear a sign 'Bws Gwynedd' for the western regions and 'Bws Clwyd' to the east of the area. Timetable enquiries for Bws Clwyd should be directed to the Clwyd County Offices, ☎ 0352 2121, Ext 4035 In Gwynedd timetable leaflets are available for most individual regions and will be available on the buses or from Infomation Centres.

CASTLES

The heyday of castle building in North Wales was in the twelfth and thirteenth centuries and the introduction of masonry walls at that time has ensured the survival of at least some remains. Iron Age hillforts, Roman enclosures and the later mottes from before this period can be seen throughout the area, but apart from the earthworks associated with these fortifications little remains of their above-ground structures.

Many of the smaller medieval castles were constructed originally by the Welsh princes in their struggles to defend the country, at first from Norman invaders and later from the succeeding monarchs' attempts to conquer the country.

In 1272 Edward I came to the

throne of England and started a campaign to subdue the Welsh princes. By 1283 he had quashed the revolt and set about building his massive 'Ring of Steel' to subjugate the Welsh. He built new castles which could be supplied by sea and strengthened strategic Welsh fortifications.

Many of the remains seen today date from this period; some examples show the ultimate in castle building techniques and overall must constitute the finest remains within any area of Europe.

The major fortifications are generally dominant in the town or village so no addresses have been given. Most are open throughout the year, some contain small museums; some have an admission charge but the smaller sites are usually free of charge.

Beaumaris
Fine castle on low-lying site with moat.

Caernarfon
The peak of the castle builders art. Traditionally associated with the Prince of Wales.

Castell Dinas-Bran
Llangollen.
Ruins high on hill overlooking the Vale of Dee.

Castell-y-Bere
Close to Tywyn.
Beautiful setting, significant in Welsh history.

Conwy
Masterpiece of engineering, complete with town walls.

Criccieth
Welsh castle extended by Edward I.

Denbigh
Thirteenth-century, with violent history in later centuries.

Deganwy
Small Welsh fortification, on Conwy estuary.

Dolbadarn
Welsh royal castle with surviving keep close to Llanberis.

Dolwyddelan
Birthplace of Llewelyn the Great — little left.

Ewloe
Pleasant site close to English borderlands.

Flint
First of Edward's castles, on the edge of the Dee. Separate Donjon.

Harlech
Commanding position; massive walls; significant in later history.

Hawarden
Old castle with little remaining. Later mansion on site was home of Gladstone, Prime Minister to Queen Victoria.

Rhuddlan
Fine remains of significant castle. Treaty of Rhuddlan in 1277 saw surrender of Llewelyn to Edward I.

Ruthin
Baronial castle now part of hotel. Permission needed to visit.

Segontium
Roman fort on outskirts of Caernarfon.

CHURCHES AND RELIGIOUS MONUMENTS

Western Wales was influenced greatly by the Celtic saints who in the sixth and seventh centuries converted the natives to Christianity. If they had churches, little now remains. However, many are associated with wells which can be visited. In other cases it is likely that present day churches occupy the sites of earlier temporary buildings and there is little doubt that this religious connection is extremely longstanding. All abbeys or monasteries were razed to the ground on the order of Henry VII and few walls remain. More recently Welsh religion has swung towards Methodism, and most villages have a fine, sometimes almost Palladian, chapel. This information is by necessity limited to the major religious sites or ruins.

Bangor Cathedral
Monastic community founded in 525 by St Deiniol and in continuous use since then.

Basingwerk Abbey
1m north-east of Flint.
Known to have been the finest monastery in Britain. Little now remains.

Clynnog Fawr
South of Caernarfon on Pwllheli Road.
Thought to have been the Mother Church of Wales founded in 616 by St Beuno and used ever since. Other ancient sites in vicinity.

Cymer Abbey
2 miles east of Dolgellau, just off road to Barmouth.
Not a lot remaining but a lovely place.

Penmon Priory
Just north of Beaumaris, Anglesey. Remains are twelfth-century and still occupied. Dovecote and well reputed to be St Seriol's. Close to Puffin Island.

St Asaph Cathedral
Said to be the smallest in Britain with library and collection of Welsh and other religious papers.

St Winifride's Chapel and Well
Holywell, Clwyd.
A place of pilgrimage with curative powers. A fine example of Perpendicular work donated by Margaret Beaufort, mother of Henry VII.

Valle Crucis Abbey
$1^1/_2$ miles west of Llangollen. Remains of Cistercian abbey in beautiful situation.

FISHING

In a country so well endowed with rivers, lakes and the sea there is obviously a wide variety of fishing available. It is necessary though to have the required permits for each stretch of inland water. Each small river, stream, lake, reservoir or canal falls within the boundary of the Welsh Water Authority. You must first obtain a licence from them to fish in these waters, then you must obtain a permit (usually available locally) to fish in the relevant stream or lake. Remember the rights to fish any stretch of water belong to the owner of the adjacent bank.

Welsh Water Authority Offices

Gwynedd River Division
Highfield, Caernarfon, Gwynedd
☎ (0286) 2247

Dee and Clwyd River Division
Shire Hall, Mold, Clwyd
☎ (0352) 2121

Some lakes for fishing:
Llyn Trawsfynydd
Llyn Tegid (Bala Lake)
Llyn Alaw, Anglesey
Tan-y-Grisiau Reservoir, Blaenau
    Ffestiniog
Llyn Brenig, near Denbigh
Lake Vyrnwy

Sea fishing is widespread right around the coast of North Wales, providing many varieties of fish and fishing. There are sands, piers and jetties and even rocks to provide a variation for the sea angler. Boats can be hired at several centres for the more adventurous.

The keen angler will probably already have a copy of the excellent publication by the Welsh Tourist Board. The Wales *Angling Guide* available nationally will tell you all you need to know about the inland and sea fishing available throughout Wales

GUIDED WALKS

The Snowdonia National Park offers a full range of guided walks throughout the season. They also offer many courses on subjects of interest such as local history, wildlife, mines and quarries, birdwatching, photography and painting. Many are for weekends or a full week. The programme of courses and walks is subject to revision each year. Details of both can be obtained from:

Snowdonia National Park Offices
Penrhyndeudraeth
Gwynedd LL68 6LF
☎ 0766-770274
or from any of the National Park visitor centres.

HOUSES AND GARDENS OPEN TO THE PUBLIC

Generally open daily between April and September.

Aberconwy House
(National Trust)
Conwy, junction of High Street and Castle Street.
☎ Conwy 2246
Open: daily, April-September, 10am-5.30pm.
Exhibition of Conwy history

Bodnant Gardens (National Trust)
Tal-y-Cafn, Colwyn Bay

Off A470, 5 miles south of Conwy
Beautiful gardens, some of the
best in Europe.
Open: daily, March-October,
10am-5pm

Bodrhydan Hall
Rhuddlan
3 miles south-east of Rhyl.
Open: June-September, Tuesday
and Thursday afternoons

Bryn Bras Castle
Llanrug, Caernarfon
A4086 between Caernarfon and
Llanberis
Open: Sunday and weekday
afternoons May-September; late
July and August 10.30am-5pm.
Romanesque castle in extensive
grounds

Chirk Castle (National Trust)
Off A5, $1/_2$ mile west of village
Open: April-September daily
except Monday and Saturday.
Early fortress which later became
an elegant household. Fine
wrought iron gates

Erddig House (National Trust)
Wrexham
Off A438, 1 mile south of Wrex-
ham.
Open: April-October, 12noon-
5.30pm, closed Monday.
Agricultural museum, restaurant

Gwydir Castle
Llanrwst
Off B5106 close to Llanrwst
Open: daily in summer except
Saturdays.
Historic Tudor mansion with
peacocks

Gwyrch Castle, Abergele
1 mile south-east of town centre.
☎ Abergele 825007
Open: each afternoon mid-May to
mid September. Café, walks and
amusements

Hafodty Gardens
Betws-Garmon, Caernarfon
4 miles south of Caernarfon on
A487
Open: daily, no charge but charity
collection box

Penrhyn Castle (National Trust)
Bangor
A5, one mile east of Bangor
Open: every day beginning April
to end October. April, May and
October 2-5pm; June-September
11am-5pm
☎ Bangor 53084
Magnificent neo-Norman hall,
Railway Museum and Doll
Museum.
Restaurant

Plas Mawr
Conwy
High Street.
Fine sixteenth-century house now
home of Royal Cambrian
Academy of Art

Plas Newydd (National Trust)
Llanfair PG, Anglesey
1 mile south-west of Llanfair PG
on A4080
Open: daily mid-April to end
October except Saturday,
12noon-5pm
☎ Llanfair 714795
On edge of Menai Straits, home
of Marquess of Anglesey. Military
Museum, restaurant

Plas Newydd
Llangollen
1 mile south of town centre.
Open: May-September

Plas-yn-Rhiw
On Lleyn Peninsula south of
Pwllheli, on the road to Aber-
daron.
Open: April-September daily
except Saturday.
Small seventeenth-century manor
house in beautiful setting

Portmeirion
Porthmadog
Near Minffordd, 2 miles east of
Porthmadog
Open: daily Easter-October
Italianate village in fine setting
and gardens

Smallest House
Conwy
On the quay.
Open: daily during summer

Ty Gwyn
Barmouth
On harbour front
Open: summer season
☎ 0341-422341
Medieval Tower House where
Tudor plotted to seize the throne
of England

Ty Mawr (National Trust)
Wybrnant, Gwybernant
$3^{1}/_{2}$ miles south-west of Betws-y-
Coed
Open: April-October daily except
Saturday, 12noon-5pm.
Birthplace of Bishop Morgan.
Nature trail

LEISURE CENTRES

Most have pools, squash courts,
badminton and other facilities.

Aberconwy Centre
Llandudno
☎ 0492-79771

Amlwch Leisure Centre
☎ 0407-830060

Buckley Sports Centre
☎ 0244-546458

Caernarfon Leisure Centre
☎ 0286-76451

Colwyn Bay
☎ 0492-63323

Deeside, Queensferry
☎ 0244-812311

Flint
☎ 03526-3677

Holyhead
☎ 0407-4111

Holywell
☎ 0352-712027

Mold Sports Centre
☎ 0352-56116

Plas Arthur Centre
Llangefni (Anglesey)
☎ 0248-722966

Plas Madoc Centre
Porthmadog
☎ 0978-821600

Prestatyn:
Nova Complex
☎ 07456-88021
Sports Centre
☎ 07456-5632

St Asaph
☎ 0745-583368

Wrexham:
Plas Madoc
☎ 0978-821600
Queensway
☎ 0978-355826
St Davids
☎ 0978-353792

MILLS AND CRAFTS

Many towns have a craft shop or two in the main street, while tourist attractions also usually have an associated craft shop selling locally made artefacts, so it is not feasible to list them all here. This list has therefore been restricted to places of manufacture that can be visited. There are many artisans working in North Wales who make a variety of products, and the local information office will be able to give the most up-to-date information. Below are listed some of the places to visit.

Potteries

Cae Dafydd
Llanfrothen, close to Beddgelert
Also has rare breed centre.

Conwy Potteries
Tyn-y-Coed Farm,
Glan Conwy, Colwyn Bay

Cwm Pottery
Trefor, near Caernarfon
Glazed pottery made in splendid location.

Dolwyddelan Pottery
The Old School, Dolwyddelan

Throwing, casting handling always in progress.

Llanbedrog Pottery
near Pwllheli
See a variety of processes.

Piggery Potteries
Y Glyn, Llanberis

Porthmadog Pottery
Snowdon Street, Porthmadog
Throw your own pot.

Woollen Mills and Knitwear

Bodeilio Weaving Centre
near Llangefni, Anglesey
Open: daily during summer

Brynkir Woollen Mills
Golan, near Porthmadog
Open: all year during working week

Holywell Textile Mills
Holywell
Open: all year Monday-Saturdays

Llangollen Weavers
Llangollen
Open: all year

Meirion Mills
Dinas Mawddwy

Penmachno Woollen Mill
near Betws-y-Coed
Open: all year during working hours and weekends in summer

Trefriw Woollen Mills
Llanrwst
Open: all year during working week and Saturdays and Sundays in summer.

Flour Mills

Felin Isaf
Llantsantffraid, Conwy Valley
Open: April-October, Tuesdays-Saturdays and Sunday 2.30-5.00pm.

Slate Products

Gloddfa Ganol
Blaenau Ffestiniog
See slate work direct from quarry face.

Inigo Jones
Tudor Slateworks, Groesion, near Caernarfon
Exhibition and workshops, clocks, lettercutting and old skills.

Llechwedd Slate Products
Blaenau Ffestiniog
Underground tours of mines and various products manufactured.

Other Crafts

Maes Artro
Llanbedr, near Harlech
Open every day during season and some parts throughout the year. Sells and manufactures a wide range of products.

Ruthin Craft Centre
Lon Parcwr, Ruthin
A purpose-built craft complex with fourteen different craft workers.

MUSEUMS AND ART GALLERIES

Some museums are run by the local councils and are open all year round. Privately owned ones are generally open only during summer months. Most have giftshops and cafés.

Canal Exhibition Centre
The Wharf, Llangollen
☎ 0978 860702
Open: Easter-end September
Museum of life on the narrow boat, horse drawn rides along the canal.

Conwy Valley Railway Museum
The Old Goods Yard, Betws-y-Coed
☎ 069202 568
Displays covering all aspects of railways.

Daniel Owen Centre
Earl Road, Mold
☎ Mold 4791
Art gallery as well as memorabilia of Welsh author

David Windsor Gallery
High Street, Bangor
Closed Wednesdays, Saturdays and Bank Holidays
Displays of paintings and porcelain from all over the world

Encounter, North Wales Museum of Wildlife
School Bank Road, Llanrwst
Open: summer: Monday-Saturday, 9.30am-6.30pm; winter: Monday-Friday, 10.30am-6.30pm
Collection of big game trophies and rare birds both local and from around the world

Geological Museum of Wales
Bwlch-gwyn, Wrexham
Adjacent to A525, $1/_2$ mile west of Bwlch-gwyn.

Exhibition of industrial relics and mining. Marked trail

Grange Cavern Military Museum
Holywell
Off A55 at Holway, near Holywell
Open: summer, 9am-6pm, winter, 9am-5pm
Collection of military vehicles and militaria in limestone caverns

Holyhead Maritime Museum
Rhos-y-Gaer Avenue, Holyhead
Open: daily May-September except Mondays. Open Bank Holidays

Llandudno Doll Museum
Masonic Street, Llandudno
Open: Easter-end of September, Monday-Saturday
Collection of old dolls and toy railways

Lleyn Historical and Maritime Museum
Old St Marys Church, Nefyn
Open: July-September

Lloyd George Museum
Llanystumdwy, near Criccieth
Open: May-September, 10am-5pm weekdays
Mementoes of this great man

Maelor Arts Centre
Rhosddu Road, Wrexham
☎ Wrexham 2351
Visiting exhibitions and displays

Mostyn Art Gallery
12 Vaughan Street, Llandudno
Open: April-September, 11am-6pm; October-March, 11am-5pm
Wide range of contemporary arts from Wales and abroad

Motor Museum
Pentrefelin, Llangollen
☎ 0978 860324
Working cars and garage

Museum of Childhood
Water Street, Menai Bridge, Anglesey
☎ 0248 712498
Open: Easter-October, Monday-Saturday, 10am-6pm, Sunday, 1-5pm
Collection of everying to do with children over the last 150 years

Museum of Old Welsh Country Life
Felin Faesog, Tai'n Lon, Clynnog Fawr
East of A499, 10 miles south of Caernarfon
Open: April-October, daily 10am-5pm
Folk museum in old corn mill

Museum of the North
Llanberis, Gwynedd
☎ 0286 870636
Open: May-September
New building devoted to natural environment of Snowdonia and Welsh nation

Museum of Welsh Antiquities
Fford Gwynedd, Bangor
Visiting exhibitions of painting and sculpture

Porthmadog Maritime Museum
The Harbour, Porthmadog
Open: daily April-September
Interesting display of harbour life 100 years ago. Slate quay re-created with sail ketch to explore

Rapallo House Museum and Art Gallery
Ffern Road, Llandudno
Open: April-November, Monday-Friday
Collection of paintings, sculptures, armour and weapons

The Royal Cambrian Academy of Art
Plas Mawr, Conwy
Annual summer exhibitions of Welsh artists

Segontium Roman Fort and Museum (National Trust)
1 mile south of Caernarfon on A4085
Open: mid-March-mid-October, Monday-Saturday, 9.30am-6.30pm; Sunday, 2-6.30pm; Mid-October-mid-March, Monday-Saturday, 9.30am-4pm, Sunday, 2-4pm
Archaeological finds and foundations

Seiont II Maritime Museum
Victoria Dock, Caernarfon
Open: daily Easter-September
Visit working steam boat.

Welsh Slate Museum
Llanberis
☎ 028 682 630
Open: daily, Easter, 9.30am-5.30pm; May-September, 9.30am-6.30pm
Shows how the slate was won, with original machinery and buildings

NATURE TRAILS AND RESERVES

There are innumerable nature trails and town trails throughout North Wales. Many are run by local authorities, the Forestry Commission or CEGB (at power stations). Most produce individual leaflets containing details of routes, etc. It is therefore wise to enquire locally for these.

The Welsh Tourist Board publishes a booklet available in most shops and information centres, called appropriately *Walking*, it covers most nature trails and town trails in the area.

The following bird reserves are owned or run by the RSPB or NWWT and welcome visitors. They are usually always open.

Aber Oguren
Near Penrhyn Castle.

Coed Garth Gell
Off A496 near north side of Penmaenpool toll bridge across Mawddach estuary.
Reserve and nature trail
☎ 0341 250650

Great Orme Country Park
Llandudno
Other nearby reserves at Little Orme, Rhos Point and Pensarn Beach.

Point of Air
On the Dee estuary east of Prestatyn.

Llyn Brenig
Clwyd
Off B4501 south-west of Denbigh.

Llyn Penrhyn
Anglesey
Near RAF Valley.

Lake Vyrnwy
Information centre off the B4393
Llanwddyn-Llanfyllin road.
☎ 069173 278

Penmaenpool Wildlife Centre
On A493 west of Dolgellau on
south side of toll bridge across
Mawddach estuary. Information
centre in old railway signal box.
Open: daily late May to September
☎ 0341 250650

South Stack Cliffs
Anglesey
Telescopes and remote-controlled
cameras at Ellin's Tower Information Centre.
☎ 0407 3043

OTHER PLACES OF INTEREST

Jails etc

Beaumaris Courthouse
Opposite castle entrance
Open: all year
Oldest and most original courthouse still being used in Wales

Beaumaris Jail
Church Street, Beaumaris,
Anglesey
Open: May-September, daily
11am-6pm.
Grim but interesting reminder of
prison life in the past

Fort Belan
Near Dinas Dinlle, Caernarfon
Open: May-September, daily
10am-5.30pm.
Old fort in fine setting, museums,

gift shop and flights over Snowdonia

Mines

Chwarel Hen
Llanfair, near Harlech
Open: Easter-October
Small but old mine, walk-in with
helmet and light

Chwarel Wynne
6 miles east of Chirk on Glyn
Ceiriog road, B4506.
Tours of slate mine and visitor
centre with films. Picnic site and
nature trail.

Gloddfa Ganol Slate Mine
Blaenau Festiniog
Open: Easter-October, daily
10am-5.30pm
Machinery and mill in world's
largest slate mine. Walk around
the caverns

Llechwedd Slate Caverns
Blaenau Ffestiniog
Open: March-October, daily
10am-6pm
See a quarry as it was 100 years
ago and visit the deepest caverns

Sygun Copper Mine
Close to Beddgelert
Open: daily March to September.
Guided tours of old mine shaft
with audio visual presentations
explaining early processes.

Power Stations

Dinorwig Power Station
☎ Llanberis 363
Hydro-electical pumped storage
scheme built inside a mountain.

Information centre and guided tours, Easter-September

Ffestiniog Power Station
Open: Easter-October
☏ Blaenau Ffestiniog 465
Pumped storage scheme with low and high reservoirs

Trawsfynydd Power Station
☏ Trawsfynydd 331
Nuclear power station set amidst mountains. Parties only allowed to visit.

Wylfa Power Station
Cemaes Bay, Anglesey
☏ Cemaes Bay 710471
Tours at 10.15am and 2pm
Monday-Friday, June-September
Observation tower open daily
Nuclear power station set on rugged coast

Zoos

Anglesey Sea Zoo
Brynsiecyn, Anglesey
☏ 0248-73411
Largest aquarium in Wales. Ideal for children with unique collection. Seafood centre and tea room.

Pili Palas
Porthaethwy close to Menai Bridge.
Butterflies from around the world in natural habitat. Relax in exotic surroundings.

Welsh Mountain Zoo and Botanical Gardens
Off Kings Road south of Colwyn Bay town centre.
☏ 0492-2938
Open: summer 9.30am-8pm,
winter 10am-4pm
Collection of birds of prey and animals in magnificent setting

RAILWAYS

There are several narrow gauge railways in North Wales and two lines operated by British rail that offer exciting scenery

Bala Lake Railway
Llanuwchllyn, Bala
Daily service April-September
☏ Llanuwchllyn 666
       or Bala 520226
Steam railway alongside lake, with magnificent scenery

Conwy Valley Railway Museum
Betws-y-Coed station
Open: daily 10.30am-5pm
Steam miniature railway and historical rolling stock and railway items

Fairbourne and Barmouth Steam Railway
Narrow gauge with Victorian-style stations. Runs along coast to meet ferry to Barmouth. Butterfly Safari on station.
Open: Late March-October
☏ 0341-250084

Festiniog Railway
Runs from Porthmadog to Blaenau Ffestiniog
Operates every day April-September and thereafter a limited service
☏ Porthmadog 2384
Superb run on most famous narrow gauge steam railway

Great Orme Tramway
Llandudno
Continuous daily service in
summer from town to summit

Llanberis Lake Railway
Runs alongside Llyn Padarn
through country park
Daily service April-September
☎ Llanberis 549

Llandudno Cabin Lift
Open: daily Easter-September,
weather permitting
Swiss-style trip up the Great
Orme

Llangollen Railway
Has short trips daily, on the hour,
alongside Afon Dee. Collection of
rolling stock. Special events.
Open: April-September.
☎ 0978-860951

Snowdon Mountain Railway
Llanberis to Snowdon summit
Daily service April-October,
conditions permitting
☎ Llanberis 223
Rack and pinion steam railway to
highest summit in England and
Wales

Tal-y-Llyn Railway
Wharf Station, Tywyn
Narrow gauge, with steam
locomotives, 14 mile round trip
from Tywyn to Nant Gwernol.
Museum at station.
Open: March-November.
☎ Tywyn 710472.

Welsh Highland Railway
Railway, closed in 1937, now
being restored. Short run in fine

scenery. Train sheds and
workshops.
Open: weekends, April, May,
June and September; daily in July
and August.
☎ 0766-513402

British rail operate regular
passenger services along the
North Wales coast and Holyhead.
Two branch lines are worthy of
mention because of the magnificent views and situation of the
lines:

Cambrian Coast Line
Aberystwyth to Pwllheli
Regular daily service
Follows coast across estuaries
with sea and mountain views. Can
be joined at any station en route

Conwy Valley Railway
Conwy to Blaenau Ffestiniog
Regular daily service throughout
the year
Superb run along valley and
through mountains. Can be joined
at any station en route

SWIMMING POOLS

There are public swimming pools
in many of the larger towns.
Opening times will vary, so check
before setting out.

Bangor
☎ 0248-370600

Blaenau Ffestiniog
☎ 0766-830484

Buckley
☎ 0244-544469

Connah's Quay
☎ 0244-819561

Conwy Valley
☎ 0492-640921

Corwen
☎ 0490-2600

Denbigh
☎074571-3958

Harlech
☎ 0978-780576

Llandudno
☎ 0492-78838

Ruthin
☎ 08242-3880

Wrexham
☎0978-263795

Rhyl Sun Centre: Pools, Wave
machine, family fun.
☎ 0745-31771

TOURIST INFORMATION CENTRES — GANOLFAN CROESO CYMRU

Many towns in North Wales now
have tourist offices either run by
the local council or the Regional
Tourism Council. They are able to
provide up-to-the-minute information on what is going on in the
area, local timetables and places
to visit, plus leaflets on local
nature trails and accommodation.
The staff are extremely helpful
and anxious to see that you get
the maximum benefit from your
visit to Wales. Most offices are
open throughout the summer and
are generally easy to find in the
town or village, being well
signposted.
　　There are information centres
in the following towns:

Aberdyfi
☎ 065-472321

Bangor
☎ 0248-352786

Betws-y-Coed
☎ 06902-426

Blaenau Ffestiniog
☎ 0766-830360

Caernarfon
☎ 0286-2232

Chester
☎0244-40144 & 49026

Colwyn Bay
☎ 0492-530478

Conwy
☎ 0492-592248

Dolgellau
☎ 0341 422888

Harlech
☎ 0766-780658

Holyhead
☎ 0407-2622

Holywell
☎ 0352 780144

Llanberis
☎ 0286-870765

Llanfair PG
☎ 0248-713177

Llangollen
☎0978-860828

Menai Bridge
☎ 0248-713923

Mold
☎ 0352-59331

Porthmadog
☎ 0766-512981

Prestatyn
☎ 07456-2484

Pwllheli
☎ 0758-613000

Rhyl
☎ 0745-55068

Rhos-on-Sea
☎ 0492-48778

Ruthin
☎ 08242-3992

Tywyn
☎0654-710070

Wrexham
☎ 0978-357845

Many of these offices can book
beds in the area for you.

USEFUL ADDRESSES

British Mountaineering Council,
Crawford House,
Precinct Centre,
Booth Street East,

Manchester MI3 9RZ
☎ 061 273 5835

British Tourist Authority,
64 St James Street
London SW1
☎ 01 499 9325

Camping and Caravanning Club
of Great Britain and Ireland
11 Lower Grosvenor Place
London SW1W 0EY
☎ 01 828 1012

Cyclists Touring Club
69 Meadrow
Godalming
Surrey
☎ Godalming 7217

Forestry Commission (Information)
231 Corstorphine Road
Edinburgh
EH12 7AT

National Mountaineering Centre
Plas-y-Brenin
Capel Curig
Betws-y-Coed
Gwynedd
☎ Capel Curig 214280

National Trust
36 Queen Anne's Gate
London SW1H 9AS
☎ 01 222 9251

National Trust
North Wales Regional Office
Trinity Square
Llandudno
Gwynedd LL30 2DE
☎ 0492 860123

North Wales Wildlife Trust
376 High Stree
Bangor
Gwynedd LL57 1YE

North Wales Tourist Board
77 Conway Road
Colwyn Bay
Clwyd

Outward Bound Trust
14 Oxford Street
London W1
☎ 01 637 4951

Rambler's Association
1-5 Wandsworth Road
London SW8 2LJ
☎ 01 582 6768

Royal Society for the Protection of Birds (Wales Office)
Bryn Aderyn
The Bank
Newtown
Powys SY16 2AB

Snowdonia National Park
Information Office
Penrhyndeudraeth
Gwynedd
☎ 0766 770274

Wales Tourist Board
PO Box 151
Cardiff CF5 1X5

Welsh Water Authority
Cambrian Way
Brecon
Clwyd

Youth Hostels Association
Trevelyan House
St Albans
Herts AL1 2DY
☎ St Albans 55215

VISITOR CENTRES

The Forestry Commission and the Welsh Water Authority have visitors' centres within the region. They generally have interesting exhibitions of the locality, its wildlife and history and they also provide picnic spots and marked trails for short walks with leaflets available detailing the route and what to look out for. They are well worth visiting to discover more about the area.

Forestry Commission Centres

Bod Petrual
In centre of Clocaenog Forest, 7 miles west of Ruthin on the B5105 road to Cerrig-y-Drudion. Story of forest past and present told in lovely setting.

Maesgwm Visitor Centre
In heart of Coed-y-Brenin (Forest of Kings) between Dolgellau and Trawsfynydd. Excellent centre with history of gold mining in the area and natural flora and fauna found in the forest. Lots of walks in miles of forest.

Y Stablau (The Stables)
In centre of village of Betws-y-Coed with information on Snowdonia National Park and the nearby Gwydyr Forest.
Open: daily during Easter week and from Spring Bank Holiday to autumn.

Other Forestry Commission areas worth visiting are:

Beddgelert Forest Park Campsite
Details of walks and wayfaring course within forest available from campsite shop.

Llyn Geirionydd
Off A5 between Betws-y-Coed and Capel Curig.
Picnic site at lakeside. Idyllic spot and start for walks or a cold swim.

Newborough Warren
On Anglesey, off A4080 from Llanfair PG
Superb situation looking across sea to mountains. Miles of beach. Forest located on dunes.

Tan-y-Coed
In Dyfi Forest, just off A487, 4 miles north of Machynlleth.
A picnic site in fine setting with lots of forest walks all around.

Water Authority Centres

Lake Vyrnwy, Clwyd
Close to dam, signposted from Tanat Valley and Bwlch-y-Groes. Pleasant little centre, with history of dam and local wildlife. Nature reserve around lake. Map of walks available from centre.

Llyn Alaw
Anglesey
Between A5 and Amlwch.
History of lake and the surrounding area. Fishing is available, and there are picnic spots.

Llyn Brenig, Clwyd
Signposted south of Denbigh on B4501.
Exhibition and information centre. Nature and history trails. Fly fishing, canoeing and sailing are allowed with permit. Lots to do in lovely setting.

INDEX